Wilderness Neighbors

"The nearby howl of a timber wolf, blood-quickening under the moon, woke us up sometime during the darkness. Reaching out a hand I could feel our dog Bushman in a trembling coil by my head. A wolf sounds different when you're camping alone, the only humans within miles."

Soon after they were married, magazine editor Brad Angier and his wife Vena decided to forsake city civilization and move to a log cabin deep in the Canadian wilderness. They went off to live the life of Thoreau in the woods of British Columbia. Their own story has been written before and enthusiastically received by a generation of young men and women who dream of cutting the tie that binds. Here now, are woods-lore-filled stories of the people who have been the Angiers' wilderness neighbors over the years in the vicinity of Hudson Hope on the Peace River.

In a remote and relatively unpopulated area, where distances are great, neighbors are really important — even those who live fifty miles away. True adventure tales of resourceful and enterprising souls who rely on themselves and nature's bounty, these are stories of trappers and Indians, mounties and miners, river men and frontier wives, living their lives in the uncharted green world that the Angiers call home.

Other Books by Bradford Angier

Field Guide to Medicinal Wild Plants
The Master Backwoodsman
Wilderness Wife
   (with Vena Angier)
The Freighter Travel Manual
The Home Book of Cooking Venison and Other Natural Meats
Looking for Gold
Field Guide to Edible Wild Plants
Introduction to Canoeing
   (with Zack Taylor)
Survival With Style
Wilderness Gear You Can Make Yourself
One Acre and Security
Feasting Free on Wild Edibles
How To Live in the Woods on Pennies a Day
The Art and Science of Taking to the Woods
   (with C. B. Colby)
A Star to the North
   (with Barbara Corcoran)
Home Medical Handbook
   (with E. Russel Kodet, M.D.)
More Free-For-The-Eating Wild Foods
Being Your Own Wilderness Doctor
   (with E. Russel Kodet, M.D.)
Gourmet Cooking For Free
   (in paperback as Food-From-The-Woods Cooking)
The Ghost of Spirit River
   (with Jeanne Dixon)
Skills for Taming the Wilds
Free For the Eating
Home in Your Pack
Mister Rifleman
   (with Colonel Townsend Whelen)
We Like It Wild
Wilderness Cookery
On Your Own in the Wilderness
   (with Colonel Townsend Whelen)
Living off the Country
   (in paperback as How to Stay Alive in the Woods)
How to Build Your Home in the Woods
At Home in the Woods
   (With Vena Angier)

Wilderness Neighbors

BRADFORD ANGIER

5B

A SCARBOROUGH BOOK
STEIN AND DAY/*Publishers*/New York

FIRST SCARBOROUGH BOOKS EDITION 1982

Copyright © 1979 by Bradford Angier
All rights reserved.
Designed by Ed Kaplin
Printed in the United States of America
Stein and Day/*Publishers*/Scarborough House
Briarcliff Manor, N.Y. 10510

Library of Congress Cataloging in Publication Data

Angier, Bradford.
    Wilderness neighbors.

    1.   Peace River region, B.C. and Alta.—Social
life and customs.   2.   Outdoor life—Peace River
region, B.C. and Alta.   3.   Angier, Bradford.
4.   Peace River region, B.C. and Alta.—Biography
I.   Title.
F1089.P3A53   971.23'1   78-26303
ISBN 0-8128-6100-0

For Jean Gething and all my other wonderfully individualistic neighbors in the wilderness

Contents

Illustrations

Wilderness Neighbors

| *1* |

Everyone a Character

▲

OUR NEIGHBORS who dwelt in the wilderness with us when we first took to the Far North, before the Alaska Highway was built, were all fiercely independent and self-sufficient. Each one was an individual—what the Outside would call a "character." This was to be expected, for to live on the frontier is the answer to the same human urge that made men become pioneers. Those attuned to that impulse must go, just as geese must fly north in the spring. The great majority of people, those who have become tamed, stay behind in the towns and cities. Whether an individual is vigorous or indolent, capable or unfit, admirable or lacking in morals, doesn't have much to do with it. These surface characteristics determine his way of life but not the direction of it.

The individuals who resided in these wild places, where there were more than twelve square miles for each white man and Indian, had plenty of room for their idiosyncrasies. Hudson Hope, British Columbia, when we knew it first, after a jolting 150-mile truck ride from the end of the railroad at Dawson Creek and across the creaking ice of the frozen Peace River, was a sleepy little community of the log cabins of some 38 inhabitants. The cabins were clustered, beside a great spring, around one of the red-roofed fur trading posts of the three-century-old Hudson's Bay Company on the sunny north shore of the 2,200-mile-long Peace River system.

That long waterway begins where the muddy Finlay River

rushes south down the Continental Trough and the more crystalline Parsnip River runs north to join it at the western edge of the Canadian Rockies at Mount Selwyn. From there the Peace flows serenely eastward through the entire backbone of the Rockies to the impassable 22-mile-long Rocky Mountain Canyon. We lived in that canyon.

Travelers would leave their boats above the narrow mouth of the canyon and walk the Portage, a 14-mile dirt road, to Hudson Hope. The Peace, with changes of name, then winds through nearly utter wilderness to Great Slave Lake in the Northwest Territories from whence it issues as the renowned Mackenzie River flowing north to the Arctic Ocean.

We bought our homesite at five dollars an acre and built our log cabin, corral, and cache beside a small stream, just before it cascades over a shale cutbank to the Peace 80 feet below, five miles west of town. Rocky Mountain Canyon was otherwise uninhabited except for a solitary Englishman, Dudley Shaw, who lived precisely halfway between our cabin and the Hope, where the bank sloped gradually to a broad ledge washed by the river. That's where Dudley got his water and fish.

Decades before, a cabinetmaker's apprentice living not far from London, Reginald Withers Shaw was in the habit of hiking a few miles after work in order to enjoy a few minutes of what he called angling. He made his decision one sunset. With unspoiled spaces luring him, why should he squander the vigorous years of his life just snatching briefly at freedom?

In his log manor in the foothills of the Rockies, what was he but a monarch? He plied a short trap line winters and clerked at the Hudson's Bay Company post for Dave Cuthill summers in order to earn the several hundred dollars it cost him to live regally another year. He was in his seventies, but there was an agility in his stride and a youthfulness in his smile that are absent in many a city-ridden citizen of thirty. Whereas the latter many times merely exists, our neighbor lived—inhaling fresh air, being obligated to no one, doing what he most wanted, and offering it his best.

My wife Vena met him for the first time when he was passing our expanse of south windows while checking his traps. Bushman, our Irish wolfhound, alerted us with a low-throated growl.

"Hey, Dudley," I yelled. "Come on in. The latchstring is out."

The door squeaked, and our first visitor peered in through thick-lensed spectacles that glittered in the sapphire gleam from the windows. Bushman, more formally named Dhulart dun Delgan, was quick to recognize a friend and swarmed all over him; taller than the short man, the dog threatened to bowl him over until I chained it to a birch outdoors.

Dudley stepped in, shutting out the cold behind him. Vena could see now that he was a small man, clad in a brown tweed jacket that seemed to have shrunk, and bulky woolen breeches that appeared to be too snug. The reason, she soon discovered, was not that his garb was too tight but that in cold weather he wore two of everything. It is a more practical method for an active person to stay snug, we soon learned, than the habit of shifting to weighty and burdensome winter garb.

"Cheerio," welcomed the newcomer in friendly tones that were not at all small. "Noble cabin you have here. I was prowling by to see if I'd snagged a marten and thought I'd check to see if you were bogged down."

"Vena, this is Dudley Shaw," I introduced. "He bakes the best sourdough bread in Hudson Hope. Even the women say so."

"Oh, will you teach me how?" she begged.

"I don't know about that," Dudley replied warily. "It usually takes time to get the knack. I'll be happy, though, to show you whatever I've picked up. Main thing with bread is to keep attacking."

"Have a bite with us?"

"Thanks, I've already had chow," replied the visitor. "It'll cheer me vastly to have some lap with you in maybe ten minutes, though, and powwow a bit. Have to look at a couple of traps above here. Then I'll stagger back this way."

"What does he mean by 'lap'?" Vena asked me when he'd left.

"Tea," I interpreted. "Dave, down at the Bay, was telling me that Deadly has a very appropriate vocabulary all his own."

"Deadly?" she asked, puzzled. "I thought his name was Dudley."

"As a matter of fact," I went on, "it's neither one. Fact is, it's Reginald Withers Shaw. Dave was telling me about it."

At the time when the Englishman was a cheechako, a tenderfoot as opposed to a sourdough who has spent at least one winter in the subarctic, he walked in for a job at a long since deserted gold-mining shaft near the Portage a couple of miles north of us. He had a lunch and a tea can in his knapsack, but he arrived near noon when the cook was yelling, "Come and get it or I'll throw it away." He was invited to eat as is customary, but when he saw what that worthy was heaping on each tin plate he stepped politely aside.

"That's a deadly looking mess," he whispered to the man behind him by way of explanation.

The miner let out a whoop and repeated the words for the benefit of all. The temperamental and long-abused cook accented his resignation by throwing the frying pan at the laughing offender, dislodging his kneecap. R. W. Shaw, who'd been making his own meals as does every bachelor backwoodsman, got the vacated job.

His cognomen from that moment was Deadly. This nickname naturally became Dudley over the years, or Uncle Dudley as the children affectionately knew him.

"Are you sure you've eaten?" my wife inquired anxiously when the small man came back a few minutes later, leaving his outer Indian moccasins on the stoop where the snow on them would not track up the floor nor, more importantly, melt and wet the fragrant smoke-tanned moosehide of which the footgear was made.

"Gouged myself copiously," the little bushman nodded appreciatively. "I'm glutted with vast quantities of flippers and tiger."

"Flippers?" Vena inquired.

"Flapjacks," translated Dudley Shaw.

"And tiger?" I had to ask.

"Bacon," Dudley explained. "It's striped, you know. Sounds nobler when called tiger."

After a couple of cups of tea, Dudley asked unexpectedly, "How's the enemy?"

"The what?" we said together.

"The enemy, the time," Dudley rejoindered amiably, his brown eyebrows arching over his small silver-rimmed glasses. "Got to begin rambling again before I'm glutted. Noble lap, thank you." He tamped some fresh tobacco into one of his low-bowled pipes, a collection of which we later saw upturned on a trimmed bush outside his door. "Hope to pick up some plunder for the Bay from my line up your creek. Got to stay off jawbone."

"Jawbone?" I asked, puzzled.

"Debt," Dudley paraphrased. "Ghastly."

Now that we had our cabin and cache built, we were ready to bring in our grubstake. I had dug a ventilated chamber, reached through a trapdoor in the cabin floor; then added slab shelves for food items one mustn't freeze: vegetables, eggs, canned goods, evaporated milk, and such luxuries as peaches and tomato juice. So the next morning we hiked the five miles to town. Snow is ordinarily sparse in this semi-arid area, and the occasional chinook keeps it even lower, besides which Dudley had already broken trail. There was no smoke curling from his lone stovepipe when we passed the halfway mark, so we did not disturb him.

Dave Cuthill, factor at the Hudson's Bay Company, soon had piled by the front door a great heap of sugar and flour and oatmeal sacks, Fort Garry tea, salt, pepper, coffee, baking powder, baking soda, 25-pound boxes of dried apples and such that freezing temperatures wouldn't trouble; cases of evaporated milk and of mixed canned fruits and juices, sacks of potatoes and fresh onions and the like, canned butter, and other necessities. He added several large containers of lard.

"Next fall you'll be getting a black bear or two that'll give you forty or fifty pounds of the best cooking lard you've ever eaten," he explained. "But in the meantime you'll need this. Thought about getting everything home? Here comes Ted Boynton, and he'll freight the load for you for five dollars if he isn't busy. He's on his way to the spring to water his team. Let me see."

Dave was a handsome, ruddy-faced Scotsman, wearing a tweed suit with a sweater beneath and a neat marten cap, creased in the middle so that it would fold flat in a pocket. He still had a burr in his voice, and we were on a friendly first-name basis at once. Now he stepped to the door and yelled, "Yo, Ted."

The iron shoes of two horses, a large bay and an equally big black, were clanging musically down the road, which was icy here. They pulled a creaking homemade sleigh bearing across its low sides a plank on which a round man bulged. That individual rubbed his neck with a square plump hand which had thickets of wiry black hair between the joints.

Between unbuttoned red flannel underwear and a green woolen shirt, his broad hairy chest showed above his high overalls. I couldn't make out what the two were saying, but Ted soon nodded, re-anchoring his stocking cap with one hand while pushing his short black hair beneath it with the other. Then he turned the team south down the road, beside the trading post's white picket fence that led to the river.

"He's glad of the job," Dave said, coming back with the breezy smile of a man accustomed to getting things done. "Just going to water his team first."

"Handy place for a spring," I said.

"Aye, geologists like Dr. McLearn reckon it's what's left of the original Peace River when it flowed more or less directly across the present Portage. That was before glacial moraine choked it off, and it had to cut a new channel around Bullhead Mountain where Rocky Mountain Canyon is now."

Vena had a few last-minute items to get, a Coleman gasoline pressure iron among them. By that time, Ted was back, and a little yellow mongrel circled the team officiously and snarled at our inquisitive Bushman when he ventured too near. We were soon loaded and about to be on our way when, at the last minute, Marion Cuthill, a pretty young nurse who had left the city to marry Dave, clattered down the high boardwalk between the house and the store with a bag of freshly baked hot bread which she shoved into Vena's arms.

"Come back and stay with us overnight, hear?" she urged us, joining Dave in waving godspeed.

"Dave was telling us that you've cooked for big game parties out of here in the Yukon and in the Northwest Territories," I said to Ted.

"Yep," he agreed. "Biggest outfit I was ever with was the Charles Bedeau expedition in thirty-four when Bedeau figgered he could cross the northern part of British Columbia to the Pacific with horses and Citroen half-track trucks. Didn't make it. My black horse here came from that expedition. Bedeau and his wife finally had to return by boat down the Crooked River and Peace, then across the Portage through Hudson Hope."

"What's your favorite dish?" Vena asked.

"They can keep them filly-minions and sech," Ted said. "Me,

I'm heading back north into the mountains next fall to where I can knock over a caribou. I'd roast me the tongue first, except the liver is durned near as good and won't keep so long. I'm not forgetting the leg bones, either. Ever heat them in your camp-fire, then bust them open with rocks to get at the marrow? Then you savvy what I'm palavering about."

| *2* |

How We Found
Hudson Hope

▲

PEOPLE HAVE BEEN asking us over the decades how, when we took to the woods, we decided on Hudson Hope, then a tiny wilderness nook miles from the nearest civilization.

It started, of course, with my decision to leave the city, in my case Boston. I wanted to reduce existence to its essentials and to learn what life really had to offer. Why, I thought, should Vena and I go on spending the best years of our lives earning money in order to enjoy a debatable freedom during the least valuable part?

Every one of our relatives, friends, and acquaintances thought we were crazy to quit good jobs and promising careers to go to a nigh blank space on the map. But all my life I'd been seeing the mass of men about me leading lives of not always too quiet desperation, making themselves sick so that they might lay up something against a sick day. Their incessant anxiety and strain had always seemed to me a nearly incurable form of disease. Yet they sincerely thought that no other choice lay open to them.

"But no way of thinking or doing, however ancient, can be trusted without proof," Henry Thoreau had significantly written a century before and gone ahead to prove. "What people say you can not do, you try and find you can."

As long as I can remember, my ideal was to go to the wilder-

ness and write about it. As for the writing profession, I sold my
first short story to *Boy's Life* at the age of thirteen, worked the
year around when still a youngster for ten cents a column inch
on *The Beverly Evening Times,* covering everything from foot-
ball to funerals. I wrote for such metropolitan papers as *The
Boston Globe* and *The Boston Transcript* while putting myself
through prep school and college, and then, in between free-
lancing short stories, was New England correspondent, under a
flock of different names, for every amusement industry publication from *Billboard* and *Film Daily* to the *Motion Picture Daily*
and the *Motion Picture Herald.* I worked my way up to a full-
time job as editor for the New England edition of *Boxoffice,*
including selling ads and making layouts for them for 15 percent
of the gross.

I started learning woodslore on lone camping trips near home
and by reading, reading, reading every factual outdoor book I
could lay my hands on: volumes by Colonel Townsend Whelen,
Ernest Thompson Seton, Howard Kephart, Nessmuk, Daniel
Carter Beard . . .

Then I was lucky enough to get into a troop of boy scouts,
who had their own weekend camp on Dunham Pond and summer camp at Lake Winnepesaukee, with a knowledgeable scout-
master who had sailed on one of the treasure-seeking trips to
Cocos Island. When in Boston, I spent every possible week
hunting and fishing on the Southeast Miramichi River in New
Brunswick and the Grand Cascapedia in Quebec, finding out
how to take care of myself in the outdoors. The use of firearms I
learned from thousands of rounds fired from a heavy Daisy air
rifle, before graduating to a .22 and later a scope-sighted .30-06.

My next good fortune was in finding a suitable mate, a beautiful, adaptable ballet dancer and musical show producer who
understood one great truth: "A lot of husbands and wives don't
really need one another in the cities. There are always hotels,
automats, and someone who will come in to vacuum. If you get
lonesome, there's always another man or girl in the city. At

least, we'll be going some place where you'll need me as desperately as I need you."

Vena, tops in her profession, had always lived in hotels and didn't even know how to time a soft-boiled egg. But she was eager to learn, when taught with tender loving care, and, soon knowledgeable, turned out to love the solitude and freedom perhaps even more than I. We proved early in our lives that if you have built your castles in the air, your work need not be lost. All you have to do is put the foundations under them.

But why Hudson Hope? All this time I was escaping more and more from the Hub on extended fishing and hunting trips. It was after one of the latter, when I had taken a canoe down the wild Half Moon of the upper Southwest Miramichi River in eastern Canada and was reluctantly about to return to Massachusetts, when I met Arthur C. Holman. At that time he owned an antique store in Saint John, New Brunswick.

I learned from our conversation that Holman had traveled all over the far northern wilderness, including the Northwest in which I was especially interested. For one thing, this part of the continent was still unspoiled. The hunting and fishing there were incomparable. It was a nearly untapped treasure chest. It was open compared to the thickly spruced Northeast. It was big. So I asked him the question I had put to others.

"What's the choicest bit of wilderness you've ever seen for a man and his wife to take to the woods?"

"Hudson Hope, British Columbia," Art replied with such lack of hesitation that I knew he must be right.

I did write a few letters: to the factor of the Hudson's Bay Company post there, to the owner of the little log hotel, and to the Provincial authorities in Victoria. All boded well. Then, with every single individual who knew about it saying that we were idiots of the first degree, we took the plunge. That's one decision in our lives which neither of us has even for an instant regretted.

So Art Holman, member of an aristocratic old Royalist family who is now retired in St. George, N.B., is the reason we went to this particular niche amid the mountain goats, sheep, and grizzlies in northern British Columbia, across from Alaska and just below the Yukon border.

This experienced mining engineer and surveyor had been the transit man with a survey party of twenty traveling from Pouce Coupe, B.C., to Rocky Mountain Canyon at Hudson Hope. They were scouting out a proposed extension of the Canadian Pacific Railway from Edmonton, Alberta, to take advantage of the massive coal deposits in Bullhead Mountain on whose eastern flank Hudson Hope is located. Bob Campbell was the locating engineer. Art Holman was second in command.

The end of the steel at that time, in the early thirties, was at Hythe, Alberta, some fifty miles southeast of Pouce Coupe as the eagle flies. The survey crew was taken by truck to the Kiskatinaw (Cutbank) River. They started their work from there through Sunset Prairie and Graveyard Creek, the latter having been so named because of an old cemetery there.

"The Graveyard Creek gold seekers never made it to the Klondike but were apparently hit by some kind of disease," Art Holman said. "About twenty wooden slabs were there, surrounded by a rough fence. Most of the names had been obliterated. Pulling up raspberry bushes to make a place for a tent, I turned up a rusty axhead. I was astonished to see XXX gouged into it.

"That ax came from the little Campbell factory in Saint John here, and it was probable that this had been a Saint John (or Maritime) party. If so, their relatives in the East probably never heard from any of them again. I don't think they starved, as they were less than ten miles from Moberly Lake."

The surveyors finally ran their line up the south side of the Peace River until they were opposite Bull Creek, where our homesite was later to be. There they found a sudden drop that was too big and too deep even to consider for a railroad crossing.

It was just east of here that Holman suggested that a bridge be built. This now happens to have been done, to continue an access road to Chetwynd and the Great Northern Railway.

The Campbell-Holman party then returned downriver to Maurice Creek and the Hudson Hope ferry. The men spent most of their time on the survey line, of course, and only got over to the Hope about five times in all, on Sundays and holidays. Yet the idyllic spot made a lasting impression on this astute and esthetic bushman.

All in all, three regular Canadian Pacific Railway crews worked on the survey, and an engineer named Livingston headed the entire project. Quite a few years later in Eastern Canada, this same engineer was in charge of connecting the Labrador Railroad with the great iron deposits there. Holman met him again on that job, and the two men recognized each other immediately.

Jack Thomas, familiar around Hudson Hope, was the outfitter for the Campbell-Holman crew, working with about fifteen pack horses.

About sixty of the young men "piled into Hudson Hope on Labor Day," Art tells me, "all ready for whatever deviltry we could get into. It was a red-letter day for the natives. They promptly went to their back yards, dug up what rum they had cached there, and threw a party for us.

"It was some party—everyone stinking drunk, lots of music, a few soon-forgotten fights and so on, plus a lot of big heads the next day. We clowns swiped one of the useful pottery conveniences from Bob and Ma Ferguson's beautiful little log hotel, climbed to the roof, took down the Union Jack, and left the pottery upside down at the top of the pole. What a time we drunks had getting it up there, too.

"Victoria heard about all this and sent up a constable of the B.C. Police in case there was another foofaray with these young drunks. Actually, we couldn't be blamed much, as we all had a lot of steam to let off, and there was simply nothing else to do. The men were all in their twenties, and all in all we were on survey about eight months.

"I loved the country—lots of sunshine and no mosquitoes or at least very few. Matter of fact, the only time skeeters bothered us was when we were plagued with strange red-headed ones— probably a fungus of some kind—at Graveyard Creek. But there was plenty of wildlife, good food, lots of room."

Vena and I, when we arrived at Hudson Hope nearly forty years ago, agreed with him wholeheartedly.

| *3* |

The Little Log Hotel

▲

THE NOW THRIVING city of Dawson Creek, British Columbia, where the Alaska Highway was later to start its six-months-and-one-day lunge northward to Fairbanks, was scarcely more than a few muddy streets bordered by high wooden sidewalks when we wallowed through it that February day. It was the end of the line for the lurching Muskeg Express from Edmonton. Piercing cold and a great feeling of anticipation enveloped us, even though the flat muskeg (peat bogs in the making) country through which we had jolted for a night and a day was still all about us. Where were the mountains?

We claimed the seven duffle bags that held our outfit, too much as we discovered later. All one really needs when taking to the north woods is weaponry, something like L.L. Bean rubber-bottomed leather boots, a made-to-specifications Randall knife if you can afford it, and a change of clothing including the best lightweight down-filled garments. We also fetched our six-month-old Irish wolfhound Bushman from the baggageman and kept him close on a leash. The aptly named oxford-gray pet, registered with the American Kennel Club, already weighed 100 pounds. Bushman aroused a lot of respect on this frontier where dogs worked as pack and sled animals.

The next morning, we rode the mail bus to the even smaller log cabin village of Fort St. John and crossed the frozen Peace River at Taylor Flats on the ice. A half hour of scouting the several garages found us a truck that was about to leave for

Hudson Hope on a primitive, chinook-slick trail up the snowy white shore of the Peace River.

Bushman, protected by a tarpaulin, rode behind on the high load of freight marked for our later friend, Teddy Green, Indian Agent north on the Graham River. It was to be kept in the meantime in the Hudson's Bay Company storehouse from where one of our best friends-to-be, Joe Barkley, would freight it by sleigh on a two-day trip to Ted's over a narrowly bushed trail, passable only when the muskegs were frozen. Hudson Hope, our dream, was some 150 miles by road west-northwest from where the railroad tracks ended.

"See," Vena said, sitting erectly between the driver and myself in the heat-filled cab, as the truck's four rear wheels spun toward an abrupt drop until the ruts straightened them out. Ahead the white rotundity of a mountain, that somehow inspired in us a feeling of friendship, reared into the cumulus-puffed blue sky. At last we were seeing a promise of the Rockies. A glistening array of peaks, ranges, and glaciers soon confirmed them in the ruddy sunset.

"That's Bullhead Mountain," the driver identified, double clutching. "Hudson Hope is at its foot although, oddly enough, you can't see Bullhead from there. This isn't much of a road yet, but only a few years ago there was no way into the Hope at all except by a pack-horse trail and the river. But they're mining coal on Bullhead again, and there has to be a way for the trucks."

"I thought I read somewhere that the old coal mine by some dinosaur tracks had shut down," Vena said.

"The old Gething-Aylard mine on the river is no longer being worked," the driver agreed. "But King Gething has opened another one on the near side of Bullhead, five miles in from the Portage. That's where I'll be loading for the trip back."

Moving shapes ahead, leaving a spruce-dark island for our

shore, were shadowy against the bright band of river. Bushman answered their yips with a cacophony of deep-throated barking.

"Coyotes after rabbits by the Gates," the driver said. "We'll be traveling the ice there a ways. Easier than trying to get over the Hump. Better keep your door open, too. There'll be plenty of time to jump in case the ice lets go. That light over there to the right is Guy and Myrtle Robison's."

The ice, smoothed by frozen overflow, seemed to be bending beneath the wheels. I was glad when we surged up the bank and I again felt the roughness of tawny clay ruts.

"Almost there," the driver said. "Bunking with anyone in particular?"

"We have reservations at the hotel. I hope that won't be out of your way."

"Nope, it's right across from the Bay. I'm eating and sleeping there, too, as soon as I unload. That's Aunty Mac's cabin on the left. Charlie Ruxton's is beside it."

A few lights abruptly shone below, led by the cheerful glow of a kerosene lamp in a cabin by the river bank.

Bob and Maude Ferguson, the owners, ran a scrupulously clean and strict hotel, as I learned the first night when I brought the shivering Bushman into the foyer with us, and Bob politely escorted him to a warm bed in one of the outbuildings in the fenced back yard. Some, like the Gethings, allowed dogs in their homes, but others didn't.

Bob, who was small, lean, and troubled with a bad digestion, was a hospitable but meticulous host. He was also the settlement's justice of the peace and notary public. Maude, his white-haired wife, was a substantial cook. She had worked for Ted Boynton who'd run the now closed restaurant, next-door to where in 1929 Bob had opened his log hostelry in the center of Hudson Hope. The Fergusons had given the stopping place its own water supply by tapping the large spring that gushed out of the ground across the road, supplying the community with cold and sparkling water. There were only two other wells, one at the Gethings' and one further down the road opposite Vic Peck's.

The little log hotel was a beautifully structured building. Trapper and inventor Joe McFarland, husband of Aunty Mac, had been the principal constructor. He later left for California.

Joe, a tall slim man, was most meticulous. He had put together a special tool to hew each huge spruce building log flat on both sides. This consisted of a broad ax-like plane set into a plough-like frame. Directed by two guide poles, it was pulled and repulled by horses along each well-matched log. As the walls went up, sphagnum moss, free for the gathering, was strung between each tier for insulation.

The two-story, squarish building was stained a comely brown, and was kept in condition by Bob Ferguson himself with annual applications of crankcase oil. The chinking, topped with plaster, was regularly whitewashed by Bob, too, and made an attractive structure which was later bettered by the addition of a roofed front porch.

Maude, who baked excellent bread and sold the large tan loaves to transient trappers for 25 cents apiece, decorated the windows of the lobby and dining room with fine burlap, originally made to be used by the Hudson's Bay Company to bale their fur bundles. She had sewn woven-cotton cattails on the curtains. The cushions of the homemade chairs and huge sofa were harmoniously made of the same material.

A great, aluminum-painted coal oil drum, fashioned by former Mountie and later trapper and prospector Bill Carter to accept odd chunks of wood and set by him on its side on an iron stand, warmed the building. It was helped by the large black kitchen stoves on which many a robust meal was cooked by Maude.

One of the hotel's pictures had been tastefully framed with birch bark by financier Charles Bedeau who'd stopped here with his wife after his unsuccessful attempt to go through the Laurier Pass with horses and half-tracks. It was at the Bedeau chateau in France that the Duke of Windsor and American Wally Simpson had been married.

The wranglers and other sourdoughs who had been on the trek sang a lot of tunes while they were in the Hope. One of the songs they had made up was about their return trip "along the Crooked River trail, with a pole in the hand and a kicker by the tail, singing ki yi yippee yippee yea."

Vena and I stayed at the Hudson Hope Hotel for the several days it took us to get our log cabin underway at Bull Creek up Rocky Mountain Canyon.

The Fergusons, finally armed with a liquor license, eventually sold the landmark to a business syndicate which included former Mackenzie River fur trader Noel Verville who, with his wife Alice, immediately built an incongruous but functional beer parlor and extra rooms on the west side.

By then I had successfully stalked Stone sheep on the ledges above our cabin, and we had found that to our tastes they were the best eating of any meat, wild or domestic, on the North American continent. It was near there, too, that Gary Powell— who in 1959 was fast becoming the largest and most successful outfitter for big game and photographic expeditions in the Northwest—and I hunted together on horseback.

During one of these excursions, while Gary had been courting Olive Beattie, I spotted a plump young bear below us on the south shore of the Peace River. We needed the bruin for lard as well as for meat, and I slanted downward to the north shore above it. Gary elected to work downriver a bit. A shot, echoing so that it seemed to come from the south, started the blackie swimming toward us, nearer the tall, red-haired Gary who felled it as it climbed up on the bar. My shot in the brain finished the foray.

By 1957 Gary was ranching on the side. Olive and he had long since married, although because of Jim Beattie's objections—partly because he preferred that the dark-eyed Olive, the next to the youngest of the attractive Beattie girls, stay home to work at his large Gold Bar spread—Bob Ferguson refused to perform the ceremony in Hudson Hope. The couple had to continue riding to Fort St. John. There Gary's father, the famous pioneering Red Powell who'd once bell-hopped at a hotel I was familiar with across from the South Station in Boston, headed the rugged Powell clan at Charlie Lake.

Gary, to get back to 1957, invited me to go along as wrangler on one of his professional hunts. Olive was in the party as fellow hunter and cook. She was good at both, having learned the latter art from her mother Elizabeth in the always well stocked, equipped, and peopled kitchen in the great Beattie home at Gold Bar or, as it was also known, Twenty Mile.

During the late fifties Gary was bringing his sportsmen west into the mountains from the Alaska Highway with saddle and pack horses. He has since built a lavish lodge in the wilderness west-southwest of Fort Nelson and is now serving it by planes. Both he and Olive are bush pilots.

My absence would have left Vena alone, two-and-one-half miles from our nearest neighbor. So she chose to move to town and stay with the friendly Vervilles at the little Hudson Hope Hotel. It was when the Powells and I returned to Fort St. John some three weeks later that we learned there had been a fire at the hotel the night before. It was with considerable nervousness that I drove back to the Hope with Gary and Olive the next day.

Vena, the only guest at the inn, had returned to her room early after spending the evening at Thelma Peck's, Keith Peck's wife. She wanted to shampoo her hair and wash out some clothes including the single set of pajamas she had brought with her. That was why she left all her jewelry, including her engagement and wedding rings, on the glass top of the bureau when she went to bed that night in a long black nightgown.

She was staying in the new portion of the place, at the back where her window overlooked the powerhouse and the Beatties' Hudson Hope home which had formerly belonged to Fred Gaylor, the town telegrapher. Her room had a private bath.

The holocaust started in the power shed where, in the cramped back yard, hummed the gasoline-powered electric generator. The first thing Vena knew about it was at three o'clock in the morning when Alice Verville pounded on her door, frantically yelling, "Get out, get out! The hotel's on fire."

All lights were gone, of course, and already all around there was the leaping ruddiness of flames and the choking stench of smoke. In the broken darkness and the shock of the moment, Vena got her arms into the short blue robe of her otherwise drying three-piece pajama set, somehow fumbled into a pair of stretch slippers, and left without anything else.

"Get Scotty and Art Pollon," Noel Verville was shouting at the foot of the stairs and—confused, startled, and frightened— Vena ran down the miry road toward the Gethings where the two men were living in a small cabin on Mel Kyllo's property.

The pair, once she had roused them out of their somewhat drunken slumber, took one look at the leaping flames. Mouthing expletives, they unintentionally shoved her backward into a patch of wolf willow bushes in their anxiety to get to the scene. The whole town was soon responding. Someone was driving round and round in a pickup, horn blasting.

The entire back of the dry and heavily oiled wooden structure was in flames by then, and there was concern that a number of drums of gasoline in the small yard might explode. As it happened, the tops only came off, and the fuel flared like massive torches.

There would still have been time to save Vena's belongings, but there was the general shock, the dread of possibly exploding gasoline, and the lack of light except that from the blackly smoking flames. Scotty Smith did get up to Vena's room. It was too smoky to see. Scotty found suitcases but dropped them when he discovered them empty. Some shoes clattered from the top of one of the bags. Scotty rescued several of them, none matching, but that was all.

Nearly everything went, and it was then that I realized that diamonds burn. The only jewelry that Vena and I later found in the ruins was a cabochon of nephrite jade, cut from an unusually high quality chunk I'd discovered several years before. The ring stone had lost all its greenness.

A bucket brigade from the spring across the street was soon organized. Its function, however, was to wet the adjoining building; Ted Boynton's now empty restaurant which, after the fire, the Vervilles acquired for a home and store. Luckily, the prevailing wind at Hudson Hope is downriver from the west, and it blew the heat of the blazing landmark away from the other structure. Vena, in her short silk robe and long silk nightgown, was shivering, and Myrtle Robison brought her a blanket.

Having done all they could to help Vena and to assist Noel and Alice in saving their records and personal belongings, Scotty, Art Pollon, and a few other drinkers formed a brigade of their own and lugged case after case of beer from the burning barroom to a panel truck that had appeared from somewhere. This continued until Noel, afraid of a catastrophe, called a halt.

The whole town was aghast, and the glow of the flames even brought a truck of Ardill family members, who wanted to help, from the upriver side of the Halfway River. Soon nothing remained but a smoldering ruin of timbers and melted glass in a hole in the ground.

Vena spent the rest of the night in the house of the Hudson's Bay Company which had already shifted operations to Fort St. John and had rented the property to Gary and Olive Powell. The next morning Alice Verville and Art Pollon took our Packard of the moment and Vena down to Dudley Shaw's old cabin, which we had already rebuilt and occupied, for a warm set of clothing. Big-hearted Peggy Ellis, plainly spoken and down-to-earth, saw to it that Vena and Alice had a substantial breakfast with plenty of seething black tea.

When the Powells and I got back the next day, Vena—still in shock and remembering with distress, one item after another, the loss of her irreplaceable belongings—was soon sobbing in my arms. I swiftly had her safely back with me at our cabin.

No one had been hurt. We were happily together again after a separation of nearly a month and a holocaust that none of those present would ever forget. Vena had lost her jewelry, the best of her clothing, and even a laboriously knitted woolen dress, which, in panels, needed only putting together.

Back in town, Scotty and Art became benevolent hosts for a week, which was how long the beer lasted. The next day, when Vena returned the blanket to Myrtle Robison with heartfelt thanks, she asked Myrtle where her husband Guy was.

Mrs. Robison philosophically remarked, "Over at the fire sale."

| *4* |

The Old Ferryman

▲

Vic "Pappy" Peck, one of the more colorful fixtures of Hudson Hope, was born in Missouri on October 16, 1885. The family soon moved to Nebraska. It was in Nebraska that Vic was raised and educated, and it left him ever afterward with a broad cowboy hat, a cowboy drawl, and a working cowboy's way of slouching in the saddle.

Vic told us that he rode north across the Canadian border as soon as he came of age and began homesteading near Whitecourt, Alberta. More a trapper and mountain man than a farmer, he kept on traveling west, keeping ahead of civilization as much as he could. In 1910 he proved up a homestead near Pouce Coupe, B.C. It was there, four years later, that he married Kathleen Shepherd, a trained nurse from England who chanced to be visiting relatives in the town. The ceremony took place in Grande Prairie, Alberta, in what was then a nearly empty North.

But Vic was still an outdoorsman at heart and not long afterward took Kathleen to a lone trap line by the East Pine River. The fur was thick, and Vic did well. Kathleen took almost at once to the wilderness, planting her own garden where Vic had made a clearing in the woods that were on all sides. She stored the perishables from it in a cellar Vic dug below the frostline. She also collected edible wild fruits and plants, putting up jar after jar of berries and jam and marmalade;—all the while knitting and sewing the clothing that the family needed.

She even made and beaded the family moccasins and mitts from tanned moosehides that Vic secured from the nearby Indians. The usual deal, which on occasion I've myself made, was to give a squaw two green hides and to get one smoke-tanned skin in return.

The Pecks had four tall, husky boys there in the bush, but there were only a few occasions of worry such as the day when little Keith was missing for hours. They searched frantically for him, only to discover him asleep behind a nearby log. The time arrived, after a decade in the East Pine country, when education became a necessity and the Pecks decided to move "to town." So early in 1924 a family pack train appeared across the river from Hudson Hope and signaled with a rifle shot for the ferryman.

The Pecks rode up the hill into the Hope, Vic, with his wide hat, slumped in the saddle of the leading horse. Next was Kathleen with baby Bruce in her arms. Sons Keith and Don were astride the third cayuse. Vernon, the oldest at the age of six, brought up the rear.

Hudson Hope had just been surveyed for town lots, and Vic purchased two of them on the high cutbank overlooking the river. Here, with the family helping as much as possible, he built a spacious log cabin with the best chinking I have ever seen. Kathleen, who despite her own large family immediately made herself available as a nurse for the region, told me they made it by melting glue and mixing it with sawdust from the logs.

Sheet glue, also used for stage scenery, was easily secured at that time. It was so flammable that care had to be taken in the melting, accomplished by putting fragments in an old pot and setting this in a pan of boiling water over a carefully supervised outdoor fire. The results, exceedingly durable and harmonious, were worth the trouble.

Later Vic built, between the corral and the main house, a dormitory for the four boys. As the youngsters grew into tall and husky young men, many a friendly poker game, in several of which I sat, was held here. There was also a stable and other outbuildings, plus Kathleen's large vegetable and flower garden.

It was open range in the Hudson Hope country at that time, and horses in particular, many of which wandered into town for the water of the great spring, troubled Kathleen and some of her neighbors by nipping blossoms and flower tips over the fences. She kept them, including the family stock, away as best she could. Someone threw a pan of acid on some of the more troublesome at one time, and a petition against this practice was signed by most of the natives.

Vic answered the call of the wild with another trap line. He was also an excellent hunter, securing much of his venison among the foothills behind our cabin where I also had success. Neighbors always shared any surplus. Legal seasons were not too carefully observed on the frontier in those early days, but no one ever wasted meat.

Vic trapped until 1937, when he transferred his line to Donny. Don was the most boisterous and outgoing of the Peck sons, and it was his trademark to appear at the community dances with his shirttail out. He met incoming cheechakos and visiting dignitaries, including nobility, with the same unreserved friendliness. The first time I encountered him was when he was walking across the Portage with a live marten for which Dave Cuthill, H.B.C. factor at the time, credited his account for 100 dollars.

Don, in partnership with Gary and Olive Beattie Powell, later bought Bill Keily's ranch, north of the Fort St. John road a few miles downriver from town. That arrangement between two ambitious and quick-tempered young men didn't last very long. Gary and Olive stayed on the land where they built a showplace, and both Don and Gary separately became very successful big game outfitters up the Alaska Highway, Don going the further north.

In 1937 Vic Peck became the local ferryman. He was living in an ideal spot for this, overlooking Maurice Creek which was directly across river from the Hudson Hope landing, just east of the Peck cabin, being situated where the runoff from the great town spring cascades into the Peace. Those days the ferry was an ordinary large boat, propelled by a powerful outboard motor that here is better known as a "kicker."

The ferry was used mainly by human passengers. But survey parties and others occasionally had horses to cross. The method they used was to tie the swimming lead horse to the rear of the craft with a long rope and then drive the rest of the string into the water to follow. The Peace broadened and quieted in this spot. Seldom was there any difficulty, although once Gene Boring's lead horse unfortunately drowned even though Vic had slowed his progress as much as he could without allowing the ferry to drift with the current.

A two-day trail to Moberly Lake ended directly across from the spring. Over this came the limited traffic from the south, mainly Crees with Harry Garbitt, the Scot who traded with them and who sold his furs to the local Hudson's Bay Company post. Fishermen, their thoughts on the rainbow trout and Arctic grayling whose habitat extended to the waterfall about a mile up Maurice Creek, now and then crossed and recrossed with their rods, tackle, and black gnat and brown hackle flies. Too, there were those who liked to swim at the mouth of the Creek.

Lord Rhondda and Lady Willingdon landed at Hudson Hope one day when Jean Gething happened to be down at the landing for the always exciting arrival of the former's stern-wheeling *D.A. Thomas.* The three already knew one another, so Jean walked up the hill with them toward the flat. Each time a stranger appeared, Lady Willingdon would seek his identity from Jean so as to be able to greet the individual by name. Vic Peck was watering his horse when the trio reached him.

"How do you do, Mr. Peck," she greeted him, extending her hand.

Taking it somewhat doubtfully, Vic drawled, "I don't think I know you."

"I'm Lady Willingdon."

"Oh, er. . . . How do you do," Vic gasped and somehow vanished around the corner.

The generous and efficient Kathleen Peck soon became famous as Hudson Hope's medical authority, although accidents in the self-sufficient life of the bush were as rare as sickness. The only trouble was that the sourdoughs, with their wholesome way of living, had little opportunity to build up immunities. When a newcomer arrived with a cold, the germs generally swept the community.

Later Marion Cuthill, who had met and married Dave after the latter was hospitalized Outside as a result of motorcycle injuries there, became the second trained nurse in the community until the H.B.C. rotation policy moved the Cuthills to the coast just up from Prince Rupert.

I sought Kathleen Peck's assistance only once and then completely successfully. I had been climbing a tree that overlooked a ground-trembling moose lick near the headwaters of Lynx Creek on Beryl Prairie.

I had previously lost my scope-sighted Remington .300 in the sheep-and-goat-filled mountains above Gold Bar while riding Chinook through thick, clawing brush. Unbeknownst to me, the too frail front line on the Indian-tanned moosehide scabbard I was using had broken somewhere in the bush, letting the weapon slip out. Several days of searching alone and with the help of my wife and Bobby, Jimmy, Billy, and Ruth Beattie proved fruitless, and as far as I know the rifle is still there.

So at the time of the accident I was using a rebuilt, lever-action .250-3000 which Gene Boring had traded me. The carbine had an exceptionally large and sharp front sight. It had no sling. In climbing the tree and holding the saddle gun in my right hand, progressively resting its butt on limbs, I somehow let it slip through my fingers. The front sight tore open the pouch of skin between the thumb and forefinger.

Afraid of tetanus, especially because of my close association with horses, I had hurriedly ridden back to our momentarily vacant cabin. I'd probably wrongly filled the opening with tincture of iodine, then bathed it in warm antiseptic and bandaged it as best I could. Later I found out that there has never been a remembered case of lockjaw in Hudson Hope. King Gething told me it was because we are so far North.

The next day, in any event, I rode to town and sought Mrs. Peck. Commenting that the wound should give me no trouble if I kept it clean until it healed, she sent me happily on my way, as always refusing any payment. Her diagnosis, as was generally the case, was correct, and now the scar is only very faintly

I soon sold the carbine to Noel Verville and bought the permanently scope-sighted Winchester Model 70 bolt-action .30-06 I still use.

As for the hospitable Kathleen Peck, I'll never forget her remarking after some guests had outstayed their welcome, "I was sure glad to see their backs."

There was also the amusing incident when she attended a community dance only a brief time because her false teeth were out being repaired, and she refused the offer of a sourdough friend, "Here, take mine. I hardly ever wear them, anyway."

The four Peck boys, like their father, were all good hunters. Keith, like his brother Don, became a well known outfitter and guide.

"Wolverine hard to trap?" Don said to me once at Trutch, where he had his popular stop up the Alaska Highway. "They're so smart they fool themselves. The secret is to leave one trap in the open on the tree beneath the hidden, well-baited second trap. Then, while trying to avoid the concealed trap, the wolverine will back right into the open one."

After retiring as ferryman, when the experienced riverman Billy Kruger took over, Vic spent a lot of time playing bridge. Any game he sat in was a colorful one. *Finesse* to him was *finance*. After he had held a hand well-enhanced with face cards, he'd comment, "Well, I got a flock of mallards that time."

He rode around town in a rattletrap Ford, in which he once escorted Jean Gething as far as Beryl Prairie to play bridge with Joe and Claire Barkley.

The only handicap this aging sourdough suffered was increasing deafness. But when he heard a comment, he always had a reply.

| *5* |

The Country of
Lonely Bachelors

▲

Leo Rutledge, who later became famous as one of British Columbia's more heavily booked outfitters for Stone sheep and grizzly, reached the Peace River area in 1928 at the age of 18. Born in Idaho, he had later lived in Norway for a decade. His mother and stepfather finally settled in the Grande Prairie region, not far from the Hope.

Leo was originally headed for the Mackenzie River to trap, but when he reached the town of Peace River with his outfit, there was no boat leaving for Great Slave Lake and the North.

"The steamer *D. A. Thomas* was at the landing, about to go upriver to the west," Leo told me, one evening when his wife Ethel had thoughtfully invited me to supper in town after she had caught a glimpse of me that afternoon in the nearby bush, riding and trying to gentle an unbroken and bucking horse whom I named Fireweed.

"A young fellow, whose name I've forgotten, urged me to go up the Peace with him while waiting for the Great Slave Lake boat. He got off at old Fort St. John, which was then sprawled along the river, but some instinct impelled me to keep going.

"The *D. A. Thomas,* which as you know sank some years later, was neat and shipshape. I found myself particularly interested when a string of pack horses, panniers and all, belonging to Jack Thomas was loaded on at Fort St. John bound to

Hudson Hope. My excitement kept building for some reason as we neared the Hope. Sure enough, it was certainly a pretty settlement. All the buildings were made of logs, most of them whitewashed. There were no roads, only a few pleasant footpaths from house to house among the grass and fireweed.

"Ted Boynton, cheerful and round as a good cook should be, was then running what he called the Club Café. I'll always remember one of his signs on the inner walls, 'Keep your wife as a pet and eat here.' All in all, everything I saw was good enough for me. I had reached my destination, the place having a great appeal as far as I was concerned.

"My first job was on what was called a Fresno. This was a horse-powered shovel that was being used to better the grade that climbs and curves up to the Portage. Later I hired on with Ralph Osborne who was the telegraph linesman at the time."

Part of the work was to slash away toppled trees and fallen branches as well as what is called second growth—although, as Neil Gething was always impressing on me, it might be the 100th growth—the new young poplars, willow, blue spruce, lodgepole pine, and brush that here always follow a clearing or a fire. The line of heavy wire from Hudson Hope to Fort St. John had been operating, with frequent repairs, since 1915.

"There were no bridges on the way down the north bank of the Peace and very little in the way of a trail. The Peace River was still the highway, so it was pretty difficult to get in and out of the Hope at freeze-up in the fall and breakup in the spring. Even to haul our little Fresno up some of the hills, especially the Hump a few miles east of town, we had to tie a couple of saddle horses to the pole with lariats."

The three of us paused to watch a black bear coming down the opposite side of the Peace to drink. He soon lumbered back into the bush, which was just as well for Ethel was a fine cook and she had everything hot.

"That winter I started trapping," Leo said. "My first partner was a young Beaver Indian who lived north of the river. One thing I'll never forget was cooking my first bannock when we were camping where the main trail crosses the Red River. By the way, have you ever seen the old Indian burial ground back in the bush on Beryl Prairie?"

"Yes," I said. "Vena and I rode over there from Barkleys' one morning."

"Interesting spot," Leo said. "Well, anyway, the thing is that my partner thought the whole process was pretty funny. He was right. When we first tried biting through the crust, this was so hard that we almost cracked our teeth on it. I'd cooked the frypan bread over too hot a campfire, and the inside was so soft that we ate it with spoons."

In the summer Leo Rutledge worked for the same Jack Thomas he'd met on the *D. A. Thomas,* this time freighting over the Portage. There were lots of gold-washing outfits that wanted to boat west up the Peace.

"Say, that's a beautiful sight," Leo said. "It's a lot like the Inside Passage from Seattle or Vancouver to Alaska."

"It really is," I agreed. "We went Outside the last time that way, going up the Alaska Highway with Colin Campbell and a load of King's coal. From Whitehorse, we took the narrow gauge railroad past Chilkoot Pass to Skagway, Alaska, then caught one of the Canadian Pacific ships to Vancouver."

"Yes, I heard. Anyway," Leo went on, "loading the big heavy riverboats, most of them about 40 feet long, at the landing here was a tricky business."

Leo and Jack were in the habit of backing their wagon into the Peace until the vehicle was floating. Then came the job of holding with one hand onto the reins of four horses, themselves belly-deep in the river, while you helped steady the floating wagon until the boat was maneuvered aboard. Money was pretty scarce during those Depression days, but generally some sort of a trade could be agreed upon."

The summer of 1930 was one of the busiest Leo ever put in. That was the year when petite, blue-eyed, golden-haired Ethel Haines came to Hudson Hope to stay with Mrs. Fred Gaylor, wife of the telegraph operator. Between freighting and courting Miss Haines in a country of lonely bachelors, Leo was kept pretty well occupied.

When Leo won out and the couple became engaged, the young pair traveled to Hythe and were married there in Alberta. At that time Hythe was a sort of sourdoughs' Gretna Green because of the British Columbia three-week waiting interval between the issuance of a license and marriage, impractical for individuals who did not reside near one of the B.C. licensing bureaus such as the office in Fort St. John.

"On the way back to the Hope," Ethel Rutledge told Vena and me one evening when we were having supper with them at their cabin, ideally located a few feet from the cutbank of the flat overlooking Maurice Creek, "the two of us had only one horse. So we took turns riding. It seemed that every time we encountered someone, I was floundering in two feet of snow while Leo was in the saddle getting his breath back."

The log house which the Rutledges later sold to the Red Cross, upon acquiring Dan Macdonald's ranch a few miles east of town at the same time that the Red Cross was bringing in a trained nurse, was unusually attractive.

"Being English and having traveled in Holland," Ethel told us, "I insisted on this Dutch kitchen."

It was a sun-favored room, sideboards and cupboards of a darker wood blending harmoniously with the varnished log walls. Blue and white tile enhanced the floor. On a high shelf above snowy curtains, a blue porcelain Dutch boy and girl stared at the quaffing of many a steaming cup of Fort Garry tea from the Hudson's Bay Company outpost just down the road.

Money was scarce all over Canada and the United States during the Depression years of the thirties, but in Hudson Hope one never had to go hungry. Vegetables grew large in the home gardens which everyone had, even the Bay manager. There were also never-ending quantities of edible wild vegetables, greens, and fruits. Nearly every wild or domestic food that couldn't be stored was put up in jars. Some of the more fortunate, like the Beatties at Gold Bar, had apparatuses that sealed the wares in tin cans.

Game meat, moose and deer mostly, was shared among the inhabitants. If the weather was too warm for it to hang, that went into the sealers, too. Ethel was one of those who took part in great canning bees.

Parties of women and children gathered berries, often going by boat as far down the river as Raspberry Island below Farrell Creek. The bush teemed with pickers from the early wild strawberry days until the approaching coolness instilled flavor in the dark red lowbush cranberries. The bears were ravenous in berry times, too. No inhabitant was ever hurt by them, though, although many a time an individual glanced over a high patch she was stripping to see a black bear cramming its mouth full on the other side. The bruin always dissolved into the atmosphere.

Jean Gething just told me while I was writing this volume that she recently had a visitor at Hudson Hope who asked her, "Are there really as many berries in Hudson Hope as Brad Angier writes about in his books?"

The two were about to walk across the Portage, so Jean said, "Let's see for ourselves."

That one day they found and sampled fourteen different edible wild berries, actually an unusual occurrence as the fruits generally appear at different times during the spring and summer.

"We found raspberries, strawberries, thimbleberries, saskatoons, highbush blueberries, lowbush blueberries, dewberries, red currants, smooth black currants, rough black currants, gooseberries, highbush cranberries, lowbush cranberries, which as you know are an entirely different species, and chokecherries. Pin cherries and Oregon grapes were not present along this particular stretch at the time, nor were red huckleberries and black huckleberries which grow on wooden stems."

In any event, I was vindicated.

Leo trapped winters on Kobes Creek in the upper Halfway River country and later on the picturesque Clearwater River on the south side of the Peace, deep in the Rockies. His catches of marten in particular were among the best in the Northwest.

During several of Leo's latter years there, Bobby Beattie, oldest son of Twenty-Mile Jim and Elizabeth Beattie, was his partner. They used pack dogs extensively and did very well.

"Thirteen winters on the trap line," Leo reminisced to us one dusk during tea at the Glen, after he had gone into outfitting and ranching in a big way. He reached for Ethel's hand. "Was it ever lonely!"

| *6* |

The Coal

▲

POWER, rather than fur, gold, and ranching, has always loomed as the life blood of Hudson Hope. And it all started with Neil Gething.

It was from Neil Gething, too—handsome, white-haired, skookum which in the Chinook jargon is the word for strong, patriarch of the leading Gething family—that came my first deep interest and subsequent uses and studies of both edible and medicinal wild plants. Because of this alone I can never hope to repay him, for not only is the practice money-saving and pleasant, but for anyone anywhere at any time it can mean the difference between life and death.

Not only that, but Mr. Gething first taught me the uses, delight, and practicality to be derived from the identification of many of the 2,000 stars to be seen on any clear night when the sky is not too bright with the moon or the aurora borealis.

If it hadn't been for the already learned mastery of the lore from Colonel Townsend Whelen, he would have educated me in the matter of orientation, for he was a navigator of consummate ability, on prospecting trips sometimes setting Indians right.

In fact, there was little that Neil Gething did not know in detail, and we spent many an unforgettable day together, especially when camping by ourselves. We often talked far into the night about everything from ancient Rome to the way yarrow tea will cleanse an individual's kidneys, usually ending any necessity of rolling out of one's sleeping bag in the early hours of the morning. Neil also credited yarrow with curing his arthritis. He had an encylopedic mind, yet he was a most modest gentleman, sprinkling even his most erudite conversations with "Of course, you know this already."

For years, next to Vena, Neil Gething was my closest friend in Hudson Hope. After him was his also brilliant son, King Gething, at whose personal coal mining camp—before civilization came so close that game laws became important—I often stayed and hunted meat.

Neil Gething, who came of sturdy Welsh stock with coal in their blood, was born in 1866 in Battle Creek, Michigan, where his brother, J. W. Gething, M.D., later practiced. Neil received his technical training in geology at the University of Michigan. A pioneer of Montana, Nevada, Kootenay, and Caribou silver and gold mining camps, he made and lost fortunes.

At one time Neil owned much of the original town site of Prince George, across the mountains from Hudson Hope, which land he later sold to the Grand Trunk Pacific Railroad. A candidate for the office of first mayor of Prince George, he was defeated only by the supreme efforts of W. G. Gillett. Neil was then a partner in the biggest real estate company north of Vancouver.

Mount Gething, the flat-topped and snow-covered mountain upriver from Hudson Hope and visible from the high land here, is named for him. He has been a friend and intimate of most of the geologists and surveyors who have flocked through Hudson Hope, including the famous Dr. F. H. McLearn of Ottawa who once told me he could profitably spend an entire summer chipping away at the fossils in a single large ledge by the northwest corner of Jim Beattie's Gold Bar ranch.

The sandstone riverside of the coal mine that Neil Gething originally staked in 1908 is crisscrossed with deep dinosaur tracks, in one of which Vena and I once built our noonday fire to boil the kettle for tea and to toast, on forked green willow sticks, our wild raspberry jam and peanut butter sandwiches.

The legendary John Huston, politician and editor and the first mayor of Nelson, was a partner and pal of Mr. Gething who cajoled him into starting a newspaper at Prince George. Colonel Lowery, editor of *The Greenwood Ledger* and of *The Lower's Float,* was another old friend. So was the influential George M. Murray, member of Parliament for years, our friend, and editor of Fort St. John's foremost newspaper.

The Hon. Walter C. Nicol, former Lieutenant-Governor of British Columbia and the founder of *The Vancouver Daily Province,* boarded with the Gething family at Slocan where the latter built the first hotel while Nicol was inaugurating *The Star,* a well-known weekly. Neil was among the few who put up the capital with Nicol when this brash young newspaperman from London, Ontario, launched this particular publishing venture.

Hudson Hope first saw Neil Gething in 1908 when he came by dog team from Edmonton. Heavily financed, he was looking for the high-grade bituminous first reported by Sir Alexander Mackenzie.

A great railway boom was enveloping Western Canada, and high-grade coal was not only necessary to fire the locomotives but to add much needed tonnage for the freight trains. Neil located, successfully staked and recorded, then proceeded to develop Hudson Hope's mountain of coal, Bullhead.

The assessment work needed to prove up the Bullhead claims was done mainly by Neil Gething and his older sons, who in 1919 tunneled into a vein appearing on the river by the dinosaur tracks. A couple of years later Wes and Larry Gething, helped by fellow-owner Les Aylard, worked with Neil on the assessment activities and the setting up of a permanent camp. It was that year that the first coal was shipped out, by barge, to power a gold dredge at Taylor Flats just above Fort St. John.

Additional building was completed in 1922, including a snug cabin of squared logs a short distance downriver from the mining activities, for honeymooning Les Aylard and his bride. The

small flat was later disfigured by a fire set by a disgruntled
employee who had been discharged, but the main structures
were saved.

Wes Gething, with the help of his wife's father, installed a
sawmill with a water wheel across the river on Johnson Creek
where the Gethings had additional coal stakings. Incidentally,
some twenty years later, Neil, Larry, and I were to dismantle
this mill for transporting downriver by sleigh.

During the winter, after chinooks and the freezing of the
continuous overflow of the Peace formed a smooth highway
along the sunny north shore, numerous sleigh-loads of riverside-
heaped coal were brought downriver to the Glen. This was the
first spot accessible to Hudson Hope by trail, where the cut-
banks gave way to a gradual incline to the flat above.

During the fall of 1923 some fifty tons of coal were barged
downstream toward Peace River Crossing by Neil, Wes, and
Larry Gething, Les Aylard, and Jimmy Ruxton. It was destined
for the Edmonton, Dunvegan, and British Columbia Railway.
Ruxton got off at the Hudson Hope landing. There Vesta, who
with Lillian was one of the two Gething daughters, occupied the
tent pitched in lieu of a stateroom.

The Hudson Hope coal, which proved to be less than four
percent noncombustible, was a considerable success with the
locomotives, five-and-one-half tons taking the place of the fourteen tons of the bituminous otherwise required. But still no
railroad steel came to Hudson Hope, and the sleigh-freighted
coal continued to be largely used locally until the trucks started
coming through.

Mrs. Wesley Gething, schoolteacher for years after the un-
timely death of her husband, has the whole history of the coal
and the Gething activities in scrapbook after scrapbook. The
information contained in these starts at Battle Creek, Michigan,
with accounts of early Gething tombstones, with dates in the
seventeen-hundreds.

Les Aylard and Senator Robert Green stuck it out with Neil

year after year after sufficient assessment work had been completed to meet the requirements of a Crown Grant. All these years Neil Gething pleaded, worked, and maneuvered for a railroad to come to Hudson Hope. His dream came close to fulfillment, shortly before World War II, when the Canadian Pacific Railroad sent survey crews into the region.

Neil Gething died before his own vision was nearly realized with tracks from Prince George to Fort St. John and Dawson Creek. A bridge near our original homesite, crossed by a paved road to a railroad station beyond Moberly Lake at Chetwynd, made the final connection. Other Bullhead coal was being mined before this, by King Gething on the eastern slope by special agreement with the Government and by Lloyd Gething, the family's youngest brother, in association with Bill Currie, Al Chapple, and Dawson Creek money-man Al Hughson. The latter group had a lease with Les Aylard and the other Crown Grant owners to mine up high near the head of the Canyon.

In his search for a route across the main North American continent, Alexander Mackenzie, partner in the Northwest Trading Company which later amalgamated with the H.B.C., had first mistakenly canoed down what was to become the Mackenzie River, exploring and mapping as he journeyed to the icy Arctic Ocean. He made his second attempt again from the vicinity of Great Slave Lake, this time against the current, by the river which with changes of name eventually became known as the Peace.

Mackenzie, a companion Alexander Mackay, and a half dozen voyageurs were, so far as is known, the first white men to view the Hudson Hope country. Where our second cabin was later to be, Mackenzie in his journal made the remark that here were the largest poplars he had ever seen. He was also accompanied by two Indians who served as interpreters and only to a limited extent as guides, as the young Scot was proceeding by painstaking navigation.

They came on the sun-splashed Sunday of May 19, 1793 to

where the Hope now lies. Here they saw a trail, winding westward up the bluffs, which they took to be the Portage that Indians had previously advised them to take instead of challenging the soon impassable Rocky Mountain Canyon. Mackenzie, nevertheless, decided it would be easier to take their 34-foot canoe and some ton and a half of supplies upriver.

They made it to the great dinosaur tracks and the thick seam of coal on the north bank of the river some thirteen miles upstream, the portion that I've regularly navigated myself in my homemade 13-foot Douglas fir marine plywood boat with its 10-horsepower outboard motor. It proved possible to go about a mile further. Then rapid after narrow rapid, in addition to mountainous slopes, became too much for even the hardy band. They cut their own portage across Bullhead Mountain, hauling, skidding, and carrying their load to the smooth waters above Rocky Mountain Canyon. Mackenzie made note of the coal in his journal.

From there on to the Continental Trough, where the Parsnip and Finlay rivers meet, the water flowed serenely except for two brief and navigable rapids, through the entire backbone of the Rocky Mountains. Mackenzie wisely turned south up the clearer Parsnip River. Then turning westward again and following stream after lake after stream as much as he could, Mackenzie—301 years after Columbus had happened upon the New World—became the first explorer to cross the continent north of Mexico.

Blending red pigment with grease, he recorded the event on the southeast face of a rock with the simple words: "Alexander Mackenzie, from Canada, by land, the 22nd of July, 1793."

Although the existence of coal near Hudson Hope had long been known, the Crown held its location under reserve until the three-and-one-half-million-acre Peace River Block, transferred to British Columbia by railroad interests in return for other land used to the south, had been surveyed and formally turned over to the provincial government. In 1908 Neil Gething, along with W. S. Johnson who had asbestos mines in eastern Canada, hurried from Edmonton and as soon as they reached the Peace River continued hastening, now over the ice, to stake coal claims in Rocky Mountain Canyon.

Charlie Jones and Doug Cadenhead, trapping from a small home cabin just above where the river narrows at the canyon, made the first extensive use of the coal in their fireplace. Charlie had the idea that rich deposits of flour gold were lodged among the rocks and gravel at the bottom of the canyon, believing that this had long acted as a huge sluice.

Charlie freely talked of a scheme to dam the water at the cramped mouth of the string of rapids long enough to gather some of the treasure, even cutting on a large tree there the legend, "Application for water rights, 1912. Douglas Cadenhead—Charlie Jones." The carving could still be made out until B. C. Hydro camped at the spot just before the actual construction of the present modern earth dam, one of the largest in the world.

So ardent was Charlie about his dream that when part of the bank fell in below Cache Creek, temporarily drying up the flow where it passed the old Fort St. John on the river, Frank Beaton of the H.B.C. expostulated, "That crazy coot, Charlie Jones, has gone and dammed the river. What is the Company going to say?"

The obstruction, of course, was soon washed away.

Neil once talked the captain of the old stern-wheeler, the *D. A. Thomas,* into going upriver in high water for a load of coal. The captain could have made it, too, except the boat's steering apparatus broke near an island, which was consequently named Steamboat Island.

Actually this riverboat—which, with its cabins, dining room, and dancing salon, seemed like a floating palace to the sourdoughs—was too large for the upper Peace River, although it regularly cruised to Hudson Hope. Such landings were social events in the small town which, when the land booms expired, became for years a tight and peaceful little community.

Its population, along with that of the upper Peace and the large, blank, "unsurveyed and unexplored" miles upon miles at Wicked River, harbored only one human being for every dozen square miles. It was an unspoiled paradise when first we saw it.

Vena and I were two of the possible handful of sourdoughs ever successful in venturing by foot all the way through the bottom of Rocky Mountain Canyon, a feat made possible only by the ice of an exceedingly early and cold winter. Once we rested with Bushman at a bend where the still open rapids had worn a wider passage through their rocky prison, passable here only by a deeply undercut ledge of ice over which we crawled on our stomachs.

Vein after vein of black coal, some a few yards thick and others no more than dark streaks, lay exposed on both sides of the river. We counted over fifty of them at different levels. Nearby was the perfectly chiseled head of a dog jutting from the crags above.

This was the mountain on which a Crown Grant had been awarded Neil Gething and his friends Les Aylard and State Senator Robert Green, businessmen in Victoria. The Gething and Green interests recently went to millionaire Les Aylard, who arranged to have the partnership divided into thirds. The Gething one-third is divided equally among his children, including the widow of Wesley Gething.

Neil prospected the Pine Pass area to the south, but he told me that there the seams were more broken than those on Bullhead. In any event, Neil's interest in the new town of Prince George was the result of his Hudson Hope coal knowledge. He visualized Prince George as the clearing house for the mineral and timber wealth of the northland, which prediction has largely come true.

Neil was a contemporary of J. Augustus Heinze, perhaps the most dazzling of the Kootenay millionaires. Heinze waged war with the Canadian Pacific, Wall Street, and the big banks. Neil remembered the sad end of the Kootenay magnate. Heinze boldly entered Wall Street on his own, launching a bank which failed. When he took in the fact that his empire had fallen, Heinze shot himself in the lush office of his bankrupt New York bank.

When Whittaker Wright, the English promoter, controlled Le Roe, War Eagle, and other mining holdings at Roseland, Neil Gething was in the Kootenay area. Wright fraudulently promoted companies in England, swindling both British bankers and hordes of small investors. Arrested and brought to trial, Wright committed suicide in a Bow Street court room by swallowing prussic acid.

Another part of Neil's hectic career in Roseland took place in 1900 when William Lyon Mackenzie King, destined to become one of the Dominion's great prime ministers, arrived in the mining community to settle a strike that was paralyzing the Dominion's economy.

Active in the strike were such world-famous men as Eugene V. Debs, later the Socialist presidential candidate in the United States, Big Bill Haywood who was foremost in forming the controversial Industrial Workers of the World movement and who died in Russia following the Soviet revolution, and labor agitators Pettibone and Moyer who assassinated Idaho governor Stueneberg. There, too, were the Hon. Joseph Martin, B. C. premier, and eminent railway men from the Canadian Pacific and the Great Northern.

The bloodshed and riots wrecked mines and smelters, from which developed the Consolidated Mining and Smelting Company and its expansive metalliferous enterprises at Trail.

Neil Gething's life could be the subject of a book. He heard General Ulysses Hiram Grant successfully campaign for the eighteenth presidency of the United States. He met and talked with Thomas Alva Edison when that wizard of electricity was a telegraph operator on the Grand Trunk Railway. He knew the first John D. Rockefeller.

His enthusiasm for Hudson Hope was spurred on by his friendship with Andrew Carnegie who built up a similar community of his own in the Monongahela Valley, where that river flows north to unite with the Alleghany at Pittsburgh to form the Ohio, and who built in Pennsylvania one of the world's greatest steel empires. Neil had one of the great automobile tycoons of Detroit interested in his Hudson Hope project.

But although he often reminisced about these giants of the past, he retained a youthful and progressive outlook. Carl Springer, gold mine operator in both Ontario and British Columbia, was his associate. Such bush pilots as W. Grant MacConnachie, who used to come to the Hudson Hope dances before he became involved in the presidency of the Canadian Pacific Airline, and Russ Baker of Central B. C. Airways were his good friends, as was Captain Wop May.

Neil admired B. C. Premier Byron I. Johnson, hailing him as a natural successor to Sir Richard McBride who launched the government-owned railway to the Peace River country. He at one time negotiated with Colonel Robert McCormick, publisher of *The Chicago Tribune.*

Neil Gething dreamed of a great industrial center at Hudson Hope, never tiring of emphasizing the fact that the Peace River pass is the lowest one through the Canadian Rockies. Indicating an area near Summit Lake where many a lone riverboat commenced its journey to Hudson Hope, he often declared, "The Continental Divide at this point is a wheat field."

He realized that the bituminous coal in Bullhead Mountain is similar to that of the Lackawanna Valley where he had put in his apprenticeship in coal mining. But the difficulty was that in

1892 there was no railroad within hundreds of miles of Hudson Hope.

Despite his efforts of a half century, the nearest that tracks came to Hudson Hope in his lifetime was to Dawson Creek, to which he helped his sons, King and Lloyd, get the Bullhead coal the rough 150 miles by truck. Then the Alaska Highway was started by the U. S. Army at that sparse collection of cabins. It was completed and reached Fairbanks, Alaska, in six months and one day, and the trucks began hauling coal up this lifeline to the subarctic. Truckers like our close friends Colin Campbell, Pen Powell, Ray Fells, Lee Bazeley, and Milton Vince became familiar sights in the Hope.

Lord Rhondda, Welsh coal magnate who became food controller for Great Britain during World War I, was at one time a Gething partner and spent millions trying to open up the wealth of natural resources contiguous to Hudson Hope. After his death a daughter endeavored to further the great plans for this part of the Peace River country. Both the heirs of the late Senator Robert Green and also the Gething family's close friend Les Aylard, son of Dr. George Aylard of the Comusan Coal Mines on Vancouver Island, retain important Hudson Hope interests along with the Gethings.

Neil Gething, his interest in the various sciences always keen, brought to the attention of many the myriad of three-toe dinosaur tracks in the sandstone bedrock in front of his original coal mine near water level halfway up Rocky Mountain Canyon. He discovered the skulls and ribs of mammoth creatures which roamed this part of Canada when it was a vast swamp. Anthropologists have been able to build some fascinating exhibits at the Victoria Museum in Ottawa from these remains.

He also donated many prehistoric relics to the Provincial Museum in the B. C. capital of Victoria and to the Smithsonian Institution in Washington, D. C. He once baffled scientists to whom he shipped a live lizard-like creature he'd come upon deep underground in one of his coal seams.

His tremendous vision of Hudson Hope's industrial future was about to be realized when Neil Gething's pick was broken, and the Master of all Good Miners decreed his shift had come to an end.

| 7 |

Some Merry Snow Storms

▲

VENA AND I enjoyed some merry snow storms, while poking the fire with more enthusiasm than ever. There were also electrifying days when the red alcohol in our outdoor thermometer shrank as much as 63° below zero Fahrenheit, and the aurora borealis was abroad during the long night in all the brilliant, seething, sheeting, colors of the spectrum.

We found these frigid times stimulating rather than oppressive, even though the apple-red glow of the heater wouldn't take the chill out of the little cabin we had built from the seasoned logs of former, fallen-in shacks found on our homesite.

In the city we wouldn't have been able for years to afford a home. Now we had one for exactly $48.16, with a salvaged cookstove that Dudley Shaw, with the inherent thrift of the Farther Places, had kept painstakingly oiled so that it would not rust. Our actual cash paid out was for a used Bill Carter heater, a new stovepipe, roofing paper, an expanse of secondhand windows that faced south so that we would gain all possible light, transportation, and incidentals such as nails.

Our dwelling was small, and we could hardly entertain an echo in it, but it seemed larger for being a single apartment and two-and-one-half miles from our solitary neighbor in Rocky Mountain Canyon, Dudley Shaw, who in turn lived that distance from town.

The walls, built on stone foundations set in a rectangle thawed by fires, and warmly caulked with the abundant sphagnum moss from a nearby swamp—later chinked during a warm spell with clay mixed with water to the consistency of firm dough and applied with a homemade spud—went up with astonishing swiftness. One reason for the speed was that we measured, plumbed, and leveled everything as we proceeded.

Just as our spud was a two-inch-wide, square-edged whittled blade with a two-foot handle, our plumb line was a cartridge suspended on a length of string. A long olive bottle of water with a telltale air bubble floating in it became our level.

Five more days, as the blessed chinook weather continued, and the roof and floor were in place. The only thing left to install was the door.

"Cook up some seeded high-bush cranberries with a touch of honey," goes a Hudson Hope recipe. "They make better applesauce than prunes."

Substitutes, in other words, are many in the places as yet little vexed by man. None, however, can take the place of a rugged cabin door. Ours was fashioned with a precisely measured outer layer of heavy lumber, laid vertically so that no moisture would be entrapped in the cracks. The inner thickness was spiked on horizontally. Insulation, thick asphalt-impregnated roll roofing augmented with more sphagnum moss, was sandwiched between. I used particularly heavy hinges, so that the whole would not sag, and wedged everything correctly into place before screwing them on.

I had put in a couple of evenings carving two sturdy birch catches. One of these was already screwed to the door. The other I now attached to the door frame. One end of a hand-fashioned latch was bolted freely to the door in such a way that the length lifted easily above the catches.

Then I bored a hole through the door a few inches above the catches. I shoved a long thong of moose rawhide through this, tying one end to the latch and letting the other end fall free. Then I went indoors to test the assembly. Vena was still outside.

"The latchstring is out," I called traditionally to her. "Come on in. Come on. Try it out. We're all ready for our wilderness neighbors."

She pulled the latchstring in the proper fashion, and the heavy strip of wood angled above the catches. A gust of west wind opened the portal faster than she had anticipated. It hit my head, not too hard because I had a boot in place, as she burst through followed by the enthusiastic Bushman. Arms around each other, we leaned against the north wall and admired the sun-glittering view offered by the line of four double windows.

To our right gleamed nearly a mile of the frozen wilderness river, with two gaps in the thick ice from which steam lifted. (As we discovered, when you lay down to drink, the always rushing flow was filled with tiny ice particles.) Then there was the narrowness of Box Canyon that hid the ice from our view, although we could follow the course of the river as far as Starfish Creek by the indentations of the cliffs.

Yellowish-brown shale cliffs, some 80 feet high near where our cabin stood, rose sheerly from the opposite shore. High above these a solid length of hills, emerald with spruce, curved a sheltering arm that finally extended out of sight beyond the last precipice we could glimpse.

"I intend to build me a house which will surpass any on main street in grandeur and luxury, as soon as it pleases me as much," I quoted from Thoreau's *Walden,* "and will cost me no more than my present one."

Except for its large area of glass, our cabin was similar to all the others in Hudson Hope. They varied, of course, in size and shape.

Sourdoughs, plagued by the never-ending task of getting in

their free firewood, do all they can to preserve the heat it gives. This is a habit that generally results in tiny windows. That's one thing with which we have never agreed, although if we could have afforded it we would have used thermopane—two layers of glass with an air space between. We have never sacrificed view and light for the extra perspiration it takes to fell, cut, and split the additional lodgepole pine needed because of these extra heat vents.

We were housed. We were supplied with all the necessities. We were with each other. The world still has room, we decided then, for those who prefer the unimproved works of God to the civilized savagery of the man-made cities. Our minds turned almost agonizingly toward the mass of discontented city folk who complain idly of their hard lots when, as Thoreau had noted, they might be improving them.

We needed meat, so we shot a moose. I spent the next day, my every move watched by the tidbit-gulping Bushman, butchering it, cutting it into chunks with a knife and a meat saw, and suspending the sections from a wire stretched high above the cache floor, safely out of the reach of the smaller forest folk. Later the marble-hard, frozen slabs could only be cut with a saw or ax.

We ate everything: liver, kidneys, heart, brains, and marrow. Nothing ever went to waste in our household, and we were still feeding Bushman from similarly suspended heavy sacks of dog meal.

We hungered for some vitamin-rich fruit, although my friend Vilhjalmur Stefansson, the arctic explorer, had already proved that man can obtain all the necessary vitamins and minerals from a regular diet of fresh, not oversalted, fat, rare meat of any kind. The opinion that had somehow spread that the eating of all parts of the animal is necessary, is erroneous, Stef told me. If one prefers just fat, fresh, rare steak, that will do just as well.

But we wanted the taste of fruit. Vena and I picked and

seeded a bucketful of the still clinging orangeish high-bush cranberries and reddish rose hips. By weight and size the latter are
richer in vitamin C than oranges. The raw pulp runs from 4,000
to nearly 7,000 milligrams of vitamin C per pound. Except for
the staples, which weren't too expensive, we were living to a
large extent off the country.

The woods here are open, unlike the thick forests I was used
to in the East where in some places you have to get down and
crawl to get through the small, tight spruce. But around Hudson Hope one could ride a horse almost anywhere. Where there
are precipices or jumbles of downfall, the latter mostly from the
fires the Indians and whites were always setting to clear land,
there is usually a way around.

So I bought Chinook, a herd-leading mare. A little bit later I
traded Pat Garbitt for Cloud, a fast but docile gray stallion
whom we got Gene Boring to geld. Our neighbors didn't want a
stallion running with the mares on the free range, so rich in
grass and legumes that cayuses, nuzzling or pawing aside the
scant snowfall in cold weather, stayed fat off the land throughout the year.

Pat was the son of Harry Garbitt who was the H.B.C. repre-
sentative among the Cree Indians at Moberly Lake, two days
south across river. Harry, a skookum and rollicking Scot, had
married a wonderful Indian wife who, rumor had it, was a
descendant on her mother's side of the Sioux who had found
refuge in Canada following the Custer massacre.

Harry and Dave Cuthill, and any friends who might be present, had their weekly bottle of rum in the cellar of the Hudson's Bay Company store beside the coal-burning furnace.
Harry got along famously with everyone. He had a stopover
cabin on the eastern shore of Maurice Creek and was usually
able to get in regularly for mail and supplies except for the
periods each spring and fall when the river was impassable
because of treacherous ice.

I paid Ted Boynton twenty dollars for a heavy, custom-made saddle, with a comfortably high pommel and cantle, which had been given him by a dude. I traded with Dennis Metecheah, son of the Beaver chief two days north of Hudson Hope, for a bridle. I was able to obtain as good buys for Vena. We secured blankets for saddle pads from T. Eaton which then serviced all Canada by mail in competition with Simpson-Sears, a situation which kept the prices generally low.

We built a pole corral, and in the winter the cayuses got all the water they needed by eating snow. Other times it was easy to put ropes on the rawhide halters we kept on both and lead them to where they could drink. But you have to feed horses you keep in and use, and I bought large sheaves of oats from Matt and Erna Boe for a nickel and then a dime apiece. Chinook and Cloud ate every last straw, and the grain-replete bundles were so heavy and we handled them so carefully that one apiece in the morning and the same in the evening sufficed. Both steeds were unshod. They neck reined.

I'd had some experience ever since childhood with riding Eastern style, as had Vena. Besides, with her dancer's grace, she took to it naturally. I had one session with the bucking and heaving Chinook who had a strong feeling of independence. But she was essentially gentle and after being thrown a few times, I soon had her, head high, under obedient control. Cloud was gentle from the start. Bushman and the horses immediately became friends.

It took some abraded knees before we got accustomed to the Western way of riding, essentially sitting still through all the paces, especially trotting, by leaning back against the cantle for support and by keeping control of the animal, at the same time staying on, partly by knee pressure. We resolved it all finally with an overnight ride to the Beattie ranch with our sleeping bags, into which we rolled the essentials, tied reassuringly behind the saddles.

By the time we were back from the same 90-mile trip, we were automatically avoiding the mistakes that had made our legs raw. Leo Rutledge, Vic Peck, and other neighbors helped us in learning the proper handling techniques, such as saddling and tethering, and from then on we had no more trouble.

The horses made life a lot easier, especially when I was bringing in game. Then I often used them both as pack animals and walked, leading them. We also found that we could skid in firewood by tying whole logs to a horse's tail. First, I fastened the free end of the haul rope high on the particular tail with two half hitches, then turned the hair of the tail back and secured everything with two more half hitches. Once we were in the saddle, Chinook and Cloud, pulling as if it were a natural thing, put all their strength into skidding the burdens which sometimes got snagged and had to be chopped free.

In cold weather we burned a cord of wood a week and in summer Vena had to cook, and to secure firewood was a constant task. Vena neatly stacked the sawed and split billets for me, and it got to be a game trying to stay ahead of her.

"See," I said, "it warms us twice, once in getting the woodpile ready and the second time in the stove. And isn't it a lot more satisfying, eating a meal that has been heated by our own efforts?"

One way to recognize a cheechako in sub-zero weather, we discovered, is by the fact that the tenderfoot builds a leaping outdoor fire and sits in front of it. The sourdough, on the other hand, lounges between a smaller, longer fire and some reflective surface such as a rock.

We marveled at first at how our senses, no longer shackled by the routine of a civilized existence, found soul-stirring pleasure in merely observing the changing sky and earth. Shams and delusions are esteemed for the soundest truth, while reality is fabulous. Had Thoreau ever written anything truer? If men would observe realities only, and not permit themselves to be deluded, life would be like a fairy tale.

Cold weather doesn't close the Far North, as we discovered.

Rather, the cold opens the country by freezing streams that wind enticingly into regions not otherwise accessible. For those on snowshoes, the snow floors the thick tangles of deadwood that otherwise make a nigh-impassable jackpot of the too many partially burned expanses of the timbered subarctic wilds where, as the mixed metaphor so aptly expresses it, the hand of man has seldom set foot.

Snowfall was unusually scant in this generally semiarid region. Only for the first few weeks we were in the wilderness did we ever use snowshoes. Snow storms (there are no blizzards in Hudson Hope) were often followed by periods of extreme cold when the live trees, their sap freezing, cracked like pistol shots. People who talk literally about a Silent North, we decided, have never left civilization.

Chinooks—when the gusts of warm western air blend with the cold air as if on a winter day one were standing inside by the swinging doors of a warmly heated department store—often come after the most frigid temperatures. The chinooks melt the snow and carry away other parts of it as vapor.

Few dramas of the northern winter are as wondrous as the blue hues accompanying a chinook. We saw the damper air, which by its weight had settled in the Canyon, become so intensely blue that it seemed to be dye. Above this, the hues expanded into brilliance as they separated in varying wavelengths of powder blues, lilac, and mauve until they finally refracted into pinks.

Lofty cumulus clouds to our east, brilliant with the still concealed sun, became church-window golds and oranges against a tranquil azure sky too remote to be governed by the earthbound Canyon. Lower, wind-hurled clouds, cascading from the violet west to the carnation-scarlet east, were drenched by the stains inherent to their heights.

Chinooks in Hudson Hope begin as warm humid gales from a part of the Pacific, so warmed by the Japanese Current that most winters in the Alaska Panhandle west of us do not have such temperature extremes as those in our cherry-blossoming national capital. The dense winds give up their moisture as snow in the mountains. By the time they are blowing here, they are as balmy as spring breezes.

| *8* |

Gold Bar

▲

JAMES WALKER BEATTIE, who did more than most for Hudson Hope, first saw the town in 1913 when he came overland from Edson, due west of Edmonton, with a dozen men and wagons. Lured by tales of a golden Eldorado, he was headed for the Ominica River, west of the Canadian Rockies. He had already prospected on the Thompson River and at Tete Jaune Cache, of which he often spoke. There the tales were that nuggets lay thick in the Rocky Mountain Trench through which flowed the headwaters of the Peace.

The men were working for Jim and his partner, Alan McKinnon, who was later a fur trader at Finlay Forks where he stayed in business after the H.B.C. moved out. Jim had long been an expert with block and tackle. The party traversed the rivers by this method, finally reaching Taylor Flats where they waited for the upper Peace to freeze solidly enough to support the procession. The horses were generally working so hard that the men had to scoop away snow afternoon following afternoon so that the cayuses could more easily reach enough vetch, peavine, grass, and other fodder to keep them in good shape.

The yarns of yellow metal proved disappointing, and by spring they took their horses back to Finlay Forks, often by game trails. Here McKinnon stayed to trap and trade. Jim, his gold fever also cooled, decided to return to Hudson Hope which had remained in his dreams. He brought his horses back here in 1914 via the Laurier Pass.

It was that spring, too, that a slim and striking young blonde, Elizabeth Hausch, came downriver from Prince George. Jim won her affections, and they were married. Born in Russia of German parents, Mrs. Beattie was rugged, vigorous, healthy, hard-working, and spirited, a perfect mate for her ambitious and trailblazing husband.

Having arrived in the United States at the age of seven with her father and mother, she traveled to Canada by covered wagon and spent her first rigorous winter there in a sod house with a dirt floor. During her first winter in Hudson Hope, Mrs. Elizabeth Beattie gave birth to the first white baby in the little cluster of log cabins. Mrs. David Learmouth, wife of the manager of the Diamond P and the only other white woman in Hudson Hope, had a daughter nineteen days afterwards. Elizabeth and Jim called their youngster Louise, but she soon became better known as Toulie. She later married the personable Al Hamilton of Fort St. John.

Mrs. Beattie had already achieved another first, being the initial white woman to ride across the Portage, this on a horse owned by Harry Garbitt and Charlie Paquette who were then partners in furnishing transportation along that route.

Jim settled his new family in a cabin in the Hope and began building roads and establishing a freighting business to take advantage of them.

"When it came to finding the land near Hudson Hope where I wanted to homestead," Jim Beattie told me, "I went about it what you might call scientifically. What I did was plant potatoes at various likely spots along the north side of the river. The place where they grew best was what I chose."

This proved to be twenty miles from the end of the Portage in what was then a nearly roadless country. It was a pleasant area with, directly upriver, a steep mountainside, passable only by single lines of animals. A clear little stream flowed through the homestead the year round. In Prince George, Beattie filed on the quarter section in 1917, later acquiring additional land around it.

Finally in 1919 with five horses, sharp axes and saws, and three little girls—Mrs. Beattie having given birth to two more beauties: Mary, better known as Girlie, who eventually married flier and trucker Pen Powell of Fort St. John, and Clarisse who became the wife of Jack Baker, radio operator in the Northwest Territories and afterwards insurance executive in Fort St. John —the Beatties moved to the still largely unbroken ranch at Gold Bar.

Jim added pack horses and a riverboat to his freighting enterprises, and he engaged help. Building supplies were poled up the river from the end of the Portage. The huge amounts of grub needed to add to the meat that was shot in this great hunting country, where Stone sheep and Rocky Mountain goat came down to the cliffs overlooking the homestead and where moose and deer were thick, was brought in by pack horse.

There were more children: Bobby, who later, until he went with Leo Rutledge on the Clearwater, took over Jim's trap line; beautiful and long-legged Olive, who, at a young age, married the strapping, redheaded Gary Powell, who with her help became the most prosperous and famous big-game outfitter in northern B. C.; pretty Ruth, who wed trucker and Beryl Prairie homesteader Milton Vince; and finally the husky twin brothers, Jimmy and Billy.

Jim, a master of practical medicine, delivered some of the children himself, and Elizabeth Beattie told us she was never sick a day afterward. Jim, in fact, took care of most of the medical problems that arose at remote Gold Bar, so far from professional assistance, using overproof rum as an anesthetic and even rivaling Bill Carter at extracting teeth.

His own great trial came in 1930 when he lost a leg at a hospital. He always maintained it was a result of professional carelessness and had therefore been needless, a natural enough reaction. Afterwards, it taxed his patience and added to his temper.

Jim's convalescence after the amputation stretched on and on, and he became convinced that there were some at the hospital who'd rather see him and his problems buried and forgotten. So he returned home where his wife and daughters could nurse him with tender loving care. When Elizabeth found that pig tripe was the only thing that really agreed with him in his weakened condition, recovery came speedily. Determined and ever ambitious, he was soon again raring to work and deal.

Settling for a peg leg, Jim secured a leather cup to hold it and him firmly in his saddle. He soon became capable of going anywhere even on a spooky mount, and he could still handle a team of horses standing up. But it was Elizabeth, with the team's reins knotted around her waist, who broadcast the first wheat crop.

Jim did everything from buying gold, handling fur, and maintaining a trading post to outfitting and guiding survey and geological crews, and freighting expensive and complicated mining machinery. He had a successful family to be proud of, and with them and especially his wife always behind him, he was a one-man dynamo.

With Tommy Stott, he established another flourishing ranch, this at Twelve Mile where there was another handy creek, thus controlling for his growing herds of cattle and bands of horses an eight-mile paradise of open rolling hills, cleared for grazing land by spring fires. He usually maintained a hand at Twelve Mile Creek to keep his livestock upriver and to prevent their mingling with the Johnson stock from a few miles downstream.

The Indians had early established a precedent for these spring blazes, the redmen mainly to bring in game; for moose, deer, and other meat animals find far more feed in the succeeding luxuriant so-called second growth. In fact, I once rode past a large doe which was grazing complacently on the new plants already sprouting at the edge of one of Jim's still smoldering conflagrations.

Thus, with his becoming a justice of the peace, the postmaster at Gold Bar, a freighter for the trappers and prospectors up-river, and a host for the numerous travelers who were usually willing to put in a bit of work in return for his hospitality, James Walker Beattie came to be what some regarded as a twentieth-century laird.

He was always a cordial and helpful jack-of-all-trades—a barrel-chested, iron-muscled, shrewd, competent, dominant, personable, and ever hospitable gentleman and businessman. He was always planning far ahead and was almost always engrossed in a deal, most of which bettered the country.

Because of the help of Elizabeth and his family, Beattie had an empire at Twenty Mile which became the jumping-off spot for the upper Peace River. Many a trapper, prospector, geologist, surveyor, and passerby—generally lumped by Jim under the name *pilgrims*—was heartily welcomed, some for weeks at a time, at his feudal-like sanctuary. This was centered about a huge, two-story home, built of massive logs snaked by horses from the mountain pass just behind his property. Construction was under the guidance of master craftsman John Cramer. The oversize hen house even resembled a Swiss chalet.

Les Bazeley, who later trucked the mail from Fort St. John to Vesta Gething at Hudson Hope, told me of poling from the Portage to Twenty Mile a large riverboat, filled with flour just for mixing with the red clay a bit up the trail to chink the building. Al Meynell installed a hydraulic ram in the ever-coursing Twenty Mile Creek, ran the pipes below the frostline, and, lo! hot and cold running water and a real bathtub.

The Beatties had a large number of outbuildings, all sagaciously if inconveniently widely spaced in case of fire: a barn, stable, blacksmith shop, tack room, carpenter shop, ice house, machine shop, grainery, corrals, numerous storage sheds, other cabins, and a towering woodpile.

Jim even erected a small windmill to power the storage batteries for his sending and receiving wireless. He also had an interest in a tidy overnight cabin and barn at the head of the Portage which was often used, before trucks took over, as a stopover on the regular trips from Gold Bar to Hudson Hope.

With the help of sourdoughs working off their taxes, Beattie put bridges and a passable road from the Portage to strategically located Gold Bar. As the girls grew in strength and comeliness, they worked in the fields like men, inspiring a never-ending line of eager and efficient sourdough helpers. Well over a dozen people would normally sit around the long dining room table in the downriver end of the modern kitchen, while the presence of as many as forty for a meal was not uncommon.

"Hotcake syrup in the winter sometimes took over 1,200 pounds of sugar alone," reminisces Elizabeth Beattie. "When the Depression outside was at its height, with our own butter, cream, whole milk, eggs, home-killed meat and poultry, and jar after jar of preserves, the diet was just too rich for some of our boarders. A few broke out in boils and kept us hustling more than ever, poulticing and nursing."

Elizabeth had a bountiful cold cellar filled with vegetables, foods she and the girls had canned in tins, and with sparkling jars in which were preserves of every kind imaginable. She maintained an oversize garden from which she sold vegetables and fruits to passersby and to supplier-of-the-upper-river Dick Corliss who was a yearly purchaser, filling his great boat which had a powerful outboard motor that was handled from a seat bracketed high in the stern. Jim even devised an irrigation system for his waving fields of grain.

When I first saw Jim Beattie with his heavy wooden leg, outlined in the doorway at Gold Bar where we had stopped overnight while boating up to Finlay Forks with Billy Kruger, I thought of Robert Louis Stevenson's Long John Silver of *Treasure Island*. I remarked to Billy, "He looks like a pirate."

"He is a pirate," responded Billy admiringly.

But this *pirate,* we learned later, quit his warm bed so that my wife and I could more comfortably spend the night.

| *9* |

River Man

▲

FREDERICK JAMES CHAPMAN, veteran of two wars, came to the Peace River country about 1911, traveling by riverboat. Born in England as one of a family of twelve, he had been in Canada a half-dozen years, always pioneering westward and northward. He had been invalided out of Her Majesty's Navy at the turn of the century, at the time of the Boer War.

Being taken ill with appendicitis in spacious Hong Kong harbor the year of the Boxer Rebellion in China, Fred Chapman was moved from H.M.S. *Ocean* to the large hospital on land. Little was known about appendicitis at that time.

"Chapman," the surgeon told him, "you are a very sick man. I have read a great deal about your affliction, but I can promise nothing except to do my best. Shall I try the operation?"

In his misery Fred assented, and the procedure was a success. Although it had saved his life, the incision would not heal there in the Orient. He was sent back to England for treatment and eventual discharge. Able Seaman Chapman made a complete recovery, and when World War I blasted through Europe he had no difficulty in 1915 in joining the Canadian Army. But he was back on the Peace in 1921 to stay.

The Peace River during the early part of this century was the great highway to the West. Some dozen large boats cruised back and forth as far toward the Pacific as Hudson Hope, taking out the first livestock and grain and fur and bringing in the initial settlers, prospectors, and trappers with their outfits. With his naval background, Fred naturally went to work on these boats.

The *D. A. Thomas,* also the family name of Welsh coal ty-coon Lord Rhondda who had acquired coal interests up the Carbon River—a clear, Arctic-grayling-and-rainbow-trout-filled stream which flows north into the Peace some 30 miles above the Portage—was the largest of the craft. She was a magnificent and unusually well-appointed boat for the wilderness, with room for over 100 passengers and 200 tons of freight, drawing five feet of water loaded and two feet empty. A mail carrier, she could make the 250-mile trip from the town of Peace River to Hudson Hope in seventeen hours. Generally, however, partly because of the stops for wood to fuel her engines, the journey took several days.

There was also the smaller steamer named the *Lady Mac-worth* for Lord Rhondda's daughter. There were Peterson's *Pine Pass* and the Diamond P's *Greenfell* on which were stacked lumber from sawmills along the Peace River, together with another sawmill steamer, the *Northern Echo.* Tugs, scows, barges, and smaller freight boats also plied the waters.

Fred Chapman was a hand aboard the *Peace River,* part of the H.B.C.'s fleet which included at that time the *Weenusk* and the *Athabaska.* The Hudson's Bay Company, now over 300 years of age and the oldest trading corporation in the world, was a formidable concern, having at one time owned all Western Canada.

Art McLeod then had the contract for supplying fuel, in the form of four-foot logs, for the Bay's boats. With frequently resharpened axes and heavy crosscut saws with a handle at each end, teams of two men apiece followed the river, looking for likely stands of timber where the water was deep enough for the particular steamer to come alongside the bank. Locating such a base, they'd pitch their tents and set to cutting and stacking.

The time required for loading was about an hour, longer if it proved difficult for the steamer to berth. The going price for the woodcutter was five dollars a cord, this in the days long before power saws, a cord being a stack four-by-four-by-eight feet. The wood used was mostly lodgepole pine, some six inches in diameter.

Fred told Vena and me, one lazy afternoon when we were buying him a couple of beers at Noel Verville's barroom, that he had learned the art of river navigation from Doug Cadenhead, captain of the *Ingenika* which was named for that mineral-rich river above Finlay Forks and for the gold mining company of the same name.

Cadenhead himself had become educated the hard way, by practical experience. Doug had become interested in river navigation when he sought land near Hudson Hope and reached it with his outfit. When you entrust everything you own and love to one riverboat, he assured Fred, you get savvy in a hurry.

The year had been 1910. Cadenhead had located the land he wanted at the mouth of the Halfway River. Then he had gone back to Edmonton to ready himself for wilderness living. A portion of his preparation was the building of two boats in Edson within a couple of weeks. The craft were flat-bottomed scows, pointed at both ends. Fifty feet long, seven feet wide, and three feet deep, each was expected to transport some seven tons.

"Boats sink," the Indians at Edson told him. "Besides, how you portage?"

Nevertheless, Cadenhead traveled with them down the McLeod, Athabasca, and Lesser Slave Rivers, then across Lesser Slave Lake to Grouard. There he sold them and continued the trip to the town of Peace River by wagons, each of which rented for 20 dollars and bore a ton. Twelve men and four women were in the party, including an elderly grandmother who had to sit in her own special chair. The journey to the Halfway was completed on a stern-wheeler, two cows and some poultry being secured along the way. A team of horses was acquired later.

Once Doug Cadenhead had squatted on the land of his choosing and put in a crop, his expenses had been approximately seven thousand dollars. Finding that freighting paid better than farming, Doug began transporting the smaller but heavy privately owned riverboats of newcomers across the Portage from the landing at Hudson Hope.

"In 1915 I left the Peace for four years," Fred Chapman said, "and joined the Saskatchewan Light Infantry. In the trenches overseas a buddy of mine by the name of Davis decided to come in with me on a homestead below Hudson Hope if we ever got out of there alive. I was to go in ahead and file on a section on Jim Rose Prairie."

Once the site of a large Indian camp, this had been named for a horse wrangler who specialized in outfitting survey parties with saddle and pack horses and their gear.

"Walter King had originally filed on the land but had quit it," Fred continued. "So I got tentative title, subject to proving it up. Davis was in Southern Alberta trying to buy some cattle. The trouble was that the bottom fell out of the cattle market just about then, so instead I got a wire saying that the deal was off. Maybe it was just as well for Davis, as he later made a fortune in hogs.

"Anyway, I canceled Davis's claim. Instead of him, my neighbors were a man named Alexander on one side and Tommy Hargreaves on the other, each of us with a half section to work. On that land the third year we harvested sixty-five bushels an acre of grade number one, hard northern wheat. By this time, I was running the *Ingenika,* a scow belonging to the mining company and pushed by a tug. This sure was a change from the *D. A. Thomas* and the *Peace River.*"

"Thanks, Noel," I said to the heavy, smiling, hospitable Noel Verville who had come over to our table to see how we were doing. "More beer all around."

Noel walked around the back of the bar to fetch it.

"We built a bunkhouse on the deck," Fred Chapman continued, "right in the prow, with a partition in the middle so that we could put women passengers on one side and men on the other. That way we could accommodate ten or so passengers at a time, stowing their gear aft.

"That freight was really something. We hauled everything: mine and farm machinery, sacked grain, furniture, equipment of all kinds, poultry, regular grubstakes, produce of several sorts, and cattle and horses. I particularly remember one magnificent team of Clydesdales, heavy, feathered-legged, draft horses from Scotland."

"What was the cost for freighting?" I asked.

"Five bucks a hundred pounds upstream and three bucks for the same weight downstream," Fred said. He was a moderate-sized man, spare, well built, with closely trimmed and abundant grizzled hair and bushy dark eyebrows. "We cooked for the passengers, too. I wish they were all as easy to feed as the two Donis kids, John and Agnes, who made the whole trip on sour-dough bread and catsup. They couldn't get enough of it. Their mother and them were among the old-timers I brought in on the *Ingenika*."

Chapman's return to the upper Peace after World War I was in 1921, when he shared the deck of the *D. A. Thomas* with an old gentleman who died en route. Several other returned men and passengers were traveling at the same time, including Frank Wagner, Vern MacLean, Sam Colt, and the famous Cap Haight. The trip was a memorable one, but Fred was glad to leave the steamer at Fort St. John.

He made straight for Ivor Movick's place. Ivor, even more of an individualist than was usual, trapped with bloodhounds until Ken Birley decimated them because of the incursions they were making on his turkeys and livestock. Ivor traded and bought fur for Goffat's of the town of Peace River and ran a virtual trap-pers' rendezvous. This was at what was then the corner of Ogilvie Swamp, now the Fort St. John ball park and arena.

Fort St. John stretched along the river at that time, not north up on the flat where it has been in recent years. There were the Hudson's Bay Company, the trading post and warehouses of Revillon Frères, a telegraph office, a church, and the residence of the Bay factor, Frank Beaton. On the other side of the Peace and a bit downstream were the police barracks and the farm of Robert Ogilvie.

Upriver, where the Alaska Highway bridge and later a railroad bridge now run, was Taylor Landing, later to become long known as Taylor Flats. Now, rich because of the petroleum industry, it is the flourishing Taylor whereas formerly it was important mainly because it was there that the wide Peace was crossed, during the warm months by ferry and later on the ice.

The first settler at this south shore landing was Harry Phillips, who arrived in 1913. Then came George Daniels and George Kirkpatrick, better known respectively as Short George and Long George. All three were bachelors. Land was cleared and planted, and the flat was soon distinguished by lush green expanses of oats and wheat.

With this change to agriculture, the time came for a more suitable name. There were advocates of both Herb Phillips and an oldster who lived right on the bank, Bob DeWar. What dilemma there was ended when DeWar left the country. Then the name of Taylor Flats somehow became official and was so noted on the maps of the seemingly always present survey crews.

"The river was lively then," recollected Fred Chapman. "An enterprising gent named Dryden once brought along a Clydesdale stallion which he put at stud as a means of beefing up the draft horse population. He lived fairly well off this, along with what his wife was able to swipe from Mrs. Stewart who kept the restaurant at that time.

"Mrs. Dryden was a big-shot, unorganized type who 'did' for Mrs. Stewart in the kitchen. She found it necessary to occasionally dress her little girl—the Drydens had a houseful of children—in one of her bustier house dresses, the better to load her down in the bosom with cheese, slabs of bacon, dried fruit, rice, and whatnot.

"A chap named Teddington ran the pool hall," Fred said. "He'd steal anything you had. But the thing of it with him was that he'd cheerfully give it back if you caught him with it. His wife was just great and just as big a crook. But they were nice people. We grew very fond of them.

"The Drydens and the Teddingtons both kept cows. This particular winter I'm talking about, Teddington had his winter feed all up in the loft of his small barn. But he kept missing a little. So he got some Number Four traps—you catch wolves with Number Fours—and he put these cannily under the oat bundles at each corner of the loft. Sure enough, it worked. He caught Mrs. Dryden by the wrist. There was some kiyiing over that. You see, she'd get a ladder and just lift the odd bundle from the eaves."

Fred Chapman moved to Hudson Hope in 1925, opening an enthusiastically frequented restaurant, this after experience in an eatery for Clarke Finch in Fort St. John.

"To give you an idea of the Finch operation in the early twenties," Chapman recalled, "during the five months I was there I got cash over the counter for only two meals. The bulk of the patrons were Finch helpers for whom food was part of the deal. I figured that on my own I could make at least forty-five dollars a month. That was the wages Finch had been paying me."

Fred's new place in Hudson Hope was on a rise just upriver from where the Fergusons were later to build their log hotel. Like Movicks in Fort St. John, it soon became a regular trappers' hangout when the fur wasn't prime and at Christmas. During the remainder of the year it kept going with meals at 50 cents apiece on a help-yourself basis. Fred became famous along the river for the hearty, flavorsome batches of cookies and bread he prepared. Fred baked cookies daily in lots of from 200 to 300. He also put out two or three dozen loaves each day, selling them for 50 cents apiece.

Fred estimated that at the peak he served two to three dozen customers at each meal, although this figure fell off during the cold months when the pelts of the local fisher and marten are at their thickest and glossiest.

Trains of pack horses brought in the food staples, carrying by weight about as much rum as grub. Fred himself bent the elbow with the others, his favorite rum being Lemon Hart. Breakage was a calculated risk, Fred explained, and the strings brought along galvanized buckets so as not to *waste* any of the seepage. There never seemed to be any difficulty, when the stores arrived, in figuring out which bottles belonged to whom. There was plenty for all, especially as it was never sold to outsiders.

The rum was the potent, 40-ounce bottles of the overproof variety. The bottles lined the kitchen floor of the restaurant, along with bulging sugar and flour sacks, cases of evaporated milk (which, because of the cost of freight, sold retail during the Depression at five dollars a carton), salt, pepper, tea, coffee, and other staples, and cans of everything from tomato juice and peaches to jams.

It was not unusual for a trapper to float through the summer in an alcoholic haze unless he had stomach ulcers, and sometimes even then; all this until the time came for him to pick up his supplies in the fall and distribute them among his ring of out-cabins. A trapper like Stanley Wallace was considered to be a plutocrat because he kept a battery radio in each of his circle of stopping places. Stan liked to listen to chatter and music while he went about the never-ending chore of skinning and stretching pelts, then hanging them to dry on suspended wires, well away from the smaller varmints such as the hungry pack rats, field mice, squirrels, weasels, and the occasional chipmunk who was roused from his winter drowse.

Christmas weeks became so strenuous that Fred Chapman, joining in the festivities, usually closed down. Four years of this was enough, Fred reckoned, and he sold his business to Ted Boynton and took over a trap line on the Ottertail River. This runs into the Peace from the north, above Bob Yeomans' and Stan Wallace's old lines.

Another old-timer and friend, Billy Kruger, was Chapman's partner during the latter span. They went some 100 miles into the sheep and goat country, using a succession of overnight cabins, each near enough to another to be a haven during the short, cold, snowy days of winter. Grizzly and black bear were along the trails, so there was plenty of fat to render into shortening for cooking.

An intriguing, fossilized skeleton of a small prehistoric swamp creature on a ledge a few feet upriver from the Chapman home cabin was a source of interest to geologists and paleontologists. I first saw this one dusk, and I'll always remember the sharp shrill sound in the darkness of approaching evening of mosquito hawks diving for food from the skies high above.

Fred kept on at the Ottertail until 1946. Then he sold his trap line to tall Bruce Peck, the youngest of the Peck boys, and retired to the Beattie ranch at Gold Bar. He later moved to Hudson Hope where he became custodian of the Community's new recreation building, upriver of Stege's, where the dances and other town activities were held.

When Princess Margaret visited Fort St. John during the Centennial Year, none other than Fred Chapman was chosen to represent the old-timers of Hudson Hope.

10

The Shootings

▲

ONE OF THE foremost sourdoughs in Hudson Hope has been tall, quick, lean Guy Robison who was born in the same area as Abraham Lincoln—Palmyra in Portage County, Ohio, a mining hamlet with two stores and three saloons. In fact, Guy's wiry strength, gauntness, and regard for his fellows made him comparable to the rail-splitting president.

Born in 1874 and still active in Hudson Hope affairs at the age of 91, Guy attended school in his Ohio home town until the pioneering urge to conquer fresh country took him, at the age of 16, to North Dakota which had just been admitted as the 39th State in the Union. Arriving at the new community of Tower City, he first hired on with a contractor who was clearing land for farms. Ambitious and hard-working, Guy owned the contracting business in five years. He'd also secured a half section for himself, a section being one square mile. Here in 1896 he married.

The wanderlust was still in his blood. So he sold out and went to Arisha where he built a hotel, complete with saloon and pool hall. Finally disposing of this establishment at a good profit, he went west to Eckleston where he handled another hotel and barroom. The Far North was still alluring, especially as he watched the Canada geese flying there in their long V's in the spring. So in 1910 he settled his wife Myrtle and their five daughters, whom they both wanted to get a good education, back in Tower City and took off for the Dominion to make a new home for them.

Guy tarried in Alberta on the North Saskatchewan River at the fast-growing settlement of Edmonton. There, a more enthusiastic outdoorsman and builder than farmer, he worked on railroad grades until he had enough of a grubstake to buy his own horses and equipment. Then he freighted to Lac La Biche on the turbulent Fraser River in British Columbia.

By 1914, with the western railroad steel terminating for the time being in what is now Prince George, settlers were heading for the Peace River country. Wanting the choice of land there, Guy procured a new wagon, the sturdiest team of horses he could find, an outfit which included a five-gallon demijohn of potent White Mule, and set out north from Lac La Biche up the Fraser River.

This was then all Indian country, patrolled by the Royal North West Mounted Police who forbade firewater. Despite searches at several places, Guy was successful in smuggling the liquor until he reached the Swan River. There, lashing his horses to escape a fast-approaching Mountie, he missed the ford in the nearly trailless wilderness and encountered deep water.

Managing to save the horses and their own lives, Guy and his partner on the trip, Bill Bullen who later became a leading citizen in Dawson Creek, eventually succeeded in getting a rope on the buggy. They hauled it to safety, minus the White Mule which they vainly endeavored to fish out with a long pole before it became lost under a log jam. They also now lacked the wagon seat, the dashboard, and much of their grubstake.

Despite the almost total absence of trails, they continued north up the Pine Pass—through which now run railroad tracks and the Hart Highway—until they reached the homestead of a character called Bulldog Red near South Dawson Creek, there then being no sign of what is now a crowded and busy city.

Here Bill Bullen, who had been ailing for a while, decided to remain. So Guy rode astride his single horse until he came to Moberly Lake. Here he became friends with Charlie Paquette and Henry Farrell. Guy stayed with them until they had completed a log cabin for Paquette, then rode north to the Hope which gladdened his heart from the first.

Unfortunately, though, settlers had been coming in from the town of Peace River, and much of the land was taken. Guy located Joe Lemieux who had a team of oxen he was having trouble handling. Guy acquired these and began breaking land for Doc Fredette, mustached and solidly built veterinary surgeon whose home was the first during the new land boom in Hudson Hope which started soon after 1910. Incidentally, Fredette stayed about a dozen years, helping out in human medical care in addition to carrying on his own profession.

During the real estate rush, quite a few French Canadians located near Hudson Hope, some of them on the Portage as far west as Four Mile Creek. When the boom fizzled, the majority of the French soon left, Frank Canton in the early forties being about the last to depart. This left mainly hardy Canadian adherents with American, Scottish, English, Welsh, Ukrainian, and Scandinavian antecedents.

Guy Robison next broke fourteen acres for Jim Beattie which they later planted with oats, the first sown in this part of the North. Guy kept on clearing and breaking land, for Joe Turner and many of the old-timers, until the gold fever smote him.

With Jerry Morgan, a prospector of some experience, he rode up to Brenham Flat and there washed gold during the summer. Before the Peace froze, Guy and Jerry split their riflings, and Guy found himself with approximately a pound of the yellow metal and a goodly supply of platinum.

Guy saddled his horse, which had kept fat grazing on Brenham Flat grass, and rode toward the head of Rocky Mountain Canyon. He stopped at the old log cabin which had once belonged to Twelve-Foot Davis of Klondike fame and which later became a part of Larry Gething's trap line, turned his cayuse loose again to keep well fed on its own as was the custom of the country, suspended his saddle and bridle from a wire, walked across the Portage to Hudson Hope, built a raft, and with a steering sweep like Huckleberry Finn's drifted downriver to the town of Peace River. He got some 300 dollars for his flour gold and 40 dollars for the platinum. With the wanderlust still firing his veins, he headed back toward the prairies.

During the winter of 1917 he worked in Saskatchewan for Fred McGarvey. Here he met Morris McGarvey who was later a pioneer on the Peace in British Columbia and who remained his friend for years. The next spring Guy was back in Edmonton, looking for a job. He hired on to go to Smithers, B. C., to freight railroad ties for the Grand Trunk. From there he worked himself back up to Prince George for a spell of logging.

Hudson Hope, though, still remained foremost in his dreams. So at Giscome Portage he and a chap named Slim Estes built one of the traditional big riverboats and had it transported to Summit Lake. From there he set forth down the Crooked River, the way to the Hope from the west. Tarrying along the way at Fort McLeod, they encountered a man named Gibson, one of the old-timers at Finlay Forks, who was having difficulties with his two heavily loaded scows of trading wares.

Robison and Estes brought the scows successfully down the Parsnip River and up the Finlay River to a large slough which for a long time bore Gibson's name. Here, where Gibson had a cabin, they all worked together to make a trading post.

Gibson, representing an important fur buyer by the name of Gauphet, had ample trade goods but a scarcity of cash. Fur was bringing high prices at that time, too, and at Finlay Forks there were a lot of competitors for it. They happened to include jovial, rotund Henry Stege who later became one of the leading residents of Hudson Hope.

To get money, Guy built a boat small enough to pole and started down the Peace. At Rocky Mountain Canyon he found his saddle and cayuse, rode across the Portage to Hudson Hope, built a raft with another sweep for steering, and floated down to the town of Peace River.

Once Gauphet learned of the situation, he got together 7,000 dollars in cash, entrusted it to Guy along with 100 dollars in wages, and started him back upriver overland. At Cache Creek, Guy reencountered his old friend from Saskatchewan, Morris McGarvey. The latter was looking over the country and decided to throw in with Robison. The pair eventually poled and lined their way up the Peace, with a portage at Hudson Hope, to Finlay Forks.

There they put in a year with Gibson, the latter taking care of his post while Guy and Mac journeyed hundreds of miles with dog teams through the Wolverine Mountains and the Ingenika River area, buying prime marten, fox, wolf, fisher, wolverine, and the choice of whatever else the Indians had to offer.

During good weather, Guy put his water-borne travels to additional good use with a distinctive way of washing his underwear. He'd tie it underneath his boat in order to, as he explained, "give it a good laundering."

Guy really started putting the foundations under his air castles in 1919 when he came back to Hudson Hope and took the mail contract between there and Fort St. John, traveling by team on the river when the ice was solid and the rest of the time by pack horse up the north shore. All this time he was preparing a place for his family to rejoin him.

He homesteaded at what is called the Gates, on a flat backed by rolling hills, on his beloved Peace River seven miles downstream from Hudson Hope. There he established a little farm with a log home, spacious barn, and other outbuildings. Myrtle joined him in 1921, soon becoming a popular member of the community.

There was a lonely interval of several weeks very soon after her arrival, though, when Guy was in the hospital with a bullet wound. Guy told us the real story of this predicament, and he had witnesses.

He had been coming up the river from Peace River to Hudson Hope on the last trip in the spring of 1921. He arrived at old Fort St. John, on the river, at about four P.M. After stabling his horses, he went to the bunkhouse where he found Cap Haight, who had been a corporal in the Army, lambasting the much smaller Ed Forfar.

Guy told Cap Haight to quit, that he had hurt Forfar enough. One word led to another, and soon it was Guy and Haight who were battling. The tall, lank, wiry Guy won in a fair fight.

Haight staggered out of the bunkhouse but soon came back with a .44 revolver in his hand. He shot at Guy but missed him. Guy then tumbled behind the big barrel heater but, as he finally stood up for a look, Haight shot him in the chest. The bullet went between the ribs and came out at the back, alongside the spine but breaking no bones.

Cap Haight then wove out the door and was never seen in the Peace River country again. The rumor was that he went to Australia.

Another man who was there during the scrap got hold of a team. Those present loaded Guy into a sleigh and hurried him to Spirit River, a distance of about 130 miles over a muddy trail.

Because of a tough constitution, Guy recovered and was soon functioning once more at full strength. He was *skookum*—hale and hearty according to the Chinook jargon.

Guy's and Myrtle's hard-working and trim daughter, Iva, married and with her children—June, Dick, and Ruth Blair—soon joined them. Iva helped on Guy's trap line until, sometime later, she moved into the Hope as the wife of trail cook and restaurateur Ted Boynton.

With Myrtle and Ivy, as she became better known, to help

him with his extensive string of traps, Guy became busier than ever with prospecting, ranching, freighting, and keeping the Hudson Hope-Fort St. John road open. There the Hump was a particular problem; it was plagued with slides. Dudley Shaw kept the joke going around town, and of course it was just a joke, that Guy kept loosening rocks on Ted Boynton's half of the Hump for Ted to clear at wages and that Ted returned the favor. But the steep and unfenced Hump, often slippery with rain or chinooks, needed no help in remaining treacherous during those early days.

After Ivy had married Ted, Guy and Myrtle finally sold their ranch at the Gates. We'd been welcomed there a number of times, some of them for successful hunts in the fall when the numerous bears were fat. Guy and Myrtle moved to a white-stuccoed cottage in the middle of town, near the high cutbank with a sunny view both up and down the river. Their home was set well back from the dust and noise of the short main thoroughfare and was further secluded by a graceful grove of birches.

Before then, there had been another shooting in the Hudson Hope region. It was late in 1918 that Al McKinnon, bringing the mail from Finlay Forks, found homesteader and trapper Harry Holtmeyer dead on the floor of his cabin some four miles upriver from the Portage. There were well over a dozen bullet holes in him. His partner, Hans Christensen who lived on the next quarter section, had disappeared. Fresh snow filled in all tracks in the meantime, and a posse, of which Jim Beattie told me he had been a member, could find no signs of Christensen.

Some half-dozen years afterward Shorty Weber stopped at the trading post of Bill Innes, who'd formerly homesteaded and trapped at Hudson Hope and who was now located at Deserter Canyon on the Finlay River. Bill, guilt-ridden, told Shorty he was responsible for murdering both men. Christensen he'd weighed down in the Peace. Shorty brought the information back to the Hope. But when Ole Johnson went up to Bill's cabin past Finlay Forks, he found the door locked from the inside and the latter in there dead, a suicide.

It was theorized that the Englishman, who'd been grieving about the killing of his brother by the Germans in World War I, had considered the local German and Dane to be enemy sympathizers and had become deranged enough to murder them. The trio had been very popular locally.

The other shooting involved George Clarke who had moved onto Lynx Creek about 1919. Red squirrels have always been plentiful in the spruce swamps around the Hope, especially as their cased and cured pelts sold from a quarter to a dollar apiece. The rich dark squirrel meat is good eating, too, for those who elect not to feed it to their dogs. That's why almost all the trappers and Indians carried a light .22 rifle. Clarke, about to ride out into the bush with gentle and harmless Fred Monteith, accidentally shot himself with one while climbing aboard his horse; he died instantly.

It was unusual. The sourdoughs and Indians, both because they have become accustomed to guns and because of the special care an experienced outdoorsman instinctively takes when the nearest doctor may be a week away, have seldom carried a firearm with a cartridge in the chamber. The magazines are generally left loaded, however, for game is always apt to wander into sight. For example, I've shot bull moose for our winter's meat from my very gate and black bear, for lard and mulligans, even closer to our cabin.

| *11* |

King of the River

▲

"THE KING OF THE RIVER" as he is widely known throughout the Far North, Quentin Franklin Gething was born to Neil and Lillian Gething in New Denver, B. C., on December 22, 1908. His sagging trousers usually seemed about to slip off his narrow hips, and his shoelaces were more often than not untied, but King successfully operated his own coal mine on Bullhead Mountain for years. He became an electronic wizard, blacksmith, welder, mechanic, inventor whenever necessary, which was often, and top jack of almost every trade.

When he was still a baby, the family moved to Vancouver. He was there long enough to attend the Cecil Rhodes School and to get all he wanted of city life. King, as he was always known, forever followed his father, the great Neil Gething, from childhood onward: to Vanderhoof, to Prince George, and to Hudson Hope.

Here King helped so many sourdoughs for so many years, generally for no more payment than a cup of tea, that when civilization approached he was elected and reelected the first mayor of Hudson Hope by unassailable margins. He continued in office until resigning in 1969 because of the increasing pressure of work. He'd always kept his pledge: "I will work to serve you faithfully and will strive to my utmost to recompense you for the trust you have invested in me."

One of his typical first official acts, it so happened, was to knock the padlock off the gate in the new fence some official had placed around the great town spring, the reason for Hudson Hope's being there in the first place.

"This water has always been free to everyone," he told Vena and me, "and it's going to stay free for as long as I have anything to do with it, by Jove."

Next to his father Neil, King was for years our best friend in Hudson Hope, and we spent many a month at his homespun coal mine which was laboriously and tediously built largely out of the very forest. Here Vena, unasked, pitched in with the cooking. I, before civilization and its game laws arrived, hunted meat for the ravenous camp crew who ate virtually every part of the animals—hearts, brains, kidneys, and liver. That was when my annually renewed five-dollar Free Miner's Certificate enabled one to keep himself legally in meat.

King, a genius like his dad, never hurried and never seemed perturbed; he took unshakable and definite stands. He once displayed this trait when he appeared at his door with a rifle when a group of men came to his second camp, by an eight-and-one-half-foot coal seam, and tried to take over that mine on a technicality involving an associate. It was not the first time that outsiders had attempted to get control of King's coal holdings. He insured access to his mines, in through the forest five miles south of the Portage just beyond the Beryl Prairie turnoff, by maintaining his own road, corrugating it with beds of poles wherever necessary.

King's almost mystical trust in fate was never more marked than during some of the occasions when he set off in his riverboat up the Peace. This he usually did from the Gething overnight cabin that was a short distance from the seething narrow opening to the unnavigable Rocky Mountain Canyon.

Tranquil as usual, King once sheared the propeller pin of his big outdoor motor when starting upriver just above the whitewater. He then proceeded calmly to change it while the boat floated free. He was having a bit of difficulty. As the craft, drifting sidewise in the main current, came nearer the roaring chasm, his lone passenger became so frightened that he was kneeling and praying.

King observed in his quiet voice, "Maybe you can cooperate with the Lord better if you'll take the paddle and head us upstream. That way we'll be going in the right direction when I get this pesky pin fixed." Trembling, the man took heed of King's advice, and the kicker boomed into life feet from disaster.

Once he took an impatient businessman upriver, and this gentleman became more and more incensed at King's frequently pulling into shore to boil the kettle. The gentleman finally exploded, "My time's worth ten dollars a minute, and we've got to hurry, damn it."

King kept on the same unruffled way.

"I don't know if the chap lost any money on the trip," King told us later with a chuckle, "but, by Jove, he sure learned how to brew a good cup of tea."

King was just as calm when he was demonstrating, upriver from our cabin in the passable part of Rocky Mountain Canyon, a poorly balanced boat built by our mutual sourdough friend, Bud Stuart, who wanted to sell it. Midway during the trial run the kicker backfired and quit. King, not troubled a whit, proceeded to strip it in the comparative calmness of Box Canyon, nonchalantly lining up the irreplaceable parts on the narrow gunwale. After about fifteen minutes he had it working again. He always got out of what at the moment seemed to be unsolvable disasters.

All of us wondered what would happen if his large, broad craft with its barrels of gasoline aboard ever caught fire. We found out when this actually happened on the upper Peace. King just ambled unhurriedly through the usual clutter to the stern with an old tarpaulin and tranquilly smothered the flames, all the time singing, "Doy dé doy doy doy."

Once he, Vena, Scotty, I, and some others were enjoying a noontime meal of mulligan at his second mine when he remarked complacently, "By Jove, isn't that a bear peeking in at the window?"

I leaped up, grabbed my rifle, ran around the corner of the cookshack, and was so close that I dropped the bruin with a shot between and just above the eyes. That night we were enjoying bear liver, especially Scotty who had a prodigious appetite.

A fishing friend of ours from California, Ray Shamel, is a truly incredible person. With a new wife and two little babies, Ray underwent a vasectomy at the age of 84. Anyhow, Ray was with us once on the Peace River when the drive shaft on King's boat broke.

"By Jove," King remarked, free of any agitation, "we'll have to fix that or we'll be stranded."

"How the aitch are you going to weld it up here in the midst of nowhere?" Ray Shamel demanded without the same lack of disturbance.

"Oh, we'll just pole a bit upriver to Louie and Ed Stranberg's where they have a little handmade forge."

"And what are you going to do for blacksmith coal?"

"By Jove," King said with a chuckle, "we'll have to make some charcoal out of willow roots, won't we?"

The so-welded drive shaft held the balance of the trip.

King's durability and ingenuity showed when he was snow-shoeing. His long, seldom-stopping strides so ate up the miles that, as the day progressed, it became increasingly difficult to keep up with him.

He was frozen in more than once during his mail runs. Once, with a load of potatoes for Roy McDougal, he kept them warm by putting campfire-heated rocks amidst them and blanketing them well. After a night at Wicked River, he was stopped by the ice at the conflux of the Finlay and Parsnip Rivers in the Continental Trough. Tying up his boat and replacing the heated rocks, King proceeded by foot to Finlay Forks to get Roy to come down with a team of horses to haul the boat ashore for the winter and to fetch his potatoes safely home. Incidentally, if you've never seen a frozen potato, it resembles marble.

Then King with Frank Taylor continued on foot up the Finlay toward Fort Graham with the mail. The ground was still bare, so they brought no showshoes. The white stuff started fluffing down before they had walked more than a few miles, weighing down the small growth along the riverside and making it a nigh impassable tangle. So they headed off along what was the old Moody Trail.

Even there the snow soon became too deep to plough through, so they laid over at Joe Pierre's Indian camp where King steamed some thin green spruce poles over the campfire and bent them in the oval form of bearpaw snowshoes, stringing them with smoked moosehide strips known as babiche. The affairs were just makeshifts, but they would have to do.

"Make um Tobin Lake one big day," Joe Pierre assured them when the two set forth again.

With the soon sagging, front-heavy snowshoes it was three long, chill days before they came to Tobin Lake and the old North West Mounted Police trail that Bill Carter had helped bush out about the turn of the century.

They were soon without rations again when they found an abandoned Indian camp with a shred of meat on the bone of a moose hind quarter hanging from a tree, enough to bait a hook for fishing through the ice. They caught a couple of trout.

"By Jove," King said, "we eat again."

The only trouble is that most fish are so lean that it takes some dozen pounds of them a day to maintain one man. So they continued on, hungry, keeping up their strength with red vitamin-C-rich rose hips and frozen orange high-bush cranberries which melted on their tongues like sherbet.

By the time they reached Collins Creek, Frank Taylor managed to poke with a sharpened stick deeply enough into the frozen ground to find some beans he had cached there in plentiful times.

"What say we down them all right now, by Jove," King said philosophically, "and let tomorrow take care of itself, the way the Indians do."

So they had nothing but more berries to eat the next day. When the two of them neared Mica Meadow, they had a choice of continuing on toward the H.B.C. post or detouring a mile to the old Mica mining camp. King's hunch to do the latter paid off when they saw smoke curling up from one of the cabins' stovepipes.

"Yoooooo, the house," they yelled.

One of the Floyds opened a door and hauled them into the welcome warmth where Ernie Floyd, learning of their plight, began cooking sourdough griddle cakes as fast as the duo could down them. Their appetites sated, they continued to Fort Graham by the snow-scintillating platinum of the moon.

On one of King's many river trips along the upper Peace he enlisted the help of a church dignitary to act as bowman, although he later said with a chuckle that the churchman was "a better sky pilot than river pilot."

"Take this pole," King instructed the gentleman. "If I want you to test the depth of the water, I'll rock the boat. Then just shove the pole down straight until it hits bottom. Place your hand on it at water level and lift it to show me the depth. This will be very important.

"If you hear the kicker start to race, that'll mean we've sheared the pin in the propeller. So the water will be shallow. Just jump overboard and hold the bow until I can replace the pin."

When the boat was proceeding along a narrow stretch, the reverend was too occupied with his Bible to notice when King rocked the boat more and more urgently. So they sheared the pin.

"It won't happen again," the clergyman said, embarrassed and apologetic. "I can vouch for that, sir."

All went well until King began skillfully steering among the rocks of the Finlay Rapids, unusually rough in this stage of water. When a comber momentarily lifted the stern and started the propeller racing, Brown, who was once more occupied with his Bible, didn't stop to look but leaped overboard in about a dozen feet of water. Fortunately, the girls with them hauled him safely back into the craft.

This time he'd split his trousers at the crotch. They made camp after getting through the rapids on the south side of the Peace. Brown went into the hastily erected tent and took off his britches for the girls to sew. Because he had no spare trousers in his duffle, he donned his pajama lowers during the interval, startling riverman Dick Colliss and a boat load of University of British Columbia students. They couldn't figure out why a dignified gentleman in a dark coat and reversed collar was strolling along the shore in pajama bottoms, engrossed in his Bible.

King found it difficult to get going mornings without a cup of coffee. One dawn he was thirsting for the hot stimulant when he saw that the Reverend Brown had spread an altar cloth over the grub box and, with the help of Monica Storrs and a Miss Higgenbottom, was using it for a service. That was the last time that ever happened. Afterwards King got out the coffee-makings the night before.

I remember thinking that King looked more like a scholar than a riverman as Vena and I once started upriver with him, and the blue miles began to unfold behind us in the ever-changing artistry of God-made splendor. We'll never forget that trip nor the glittering ice specks of glaciers among the sprawling, hurtling, jutting summits and crags and snow-clad spires that spread before us in every direction, especially toward the Yukon where there were hundreds of whitened peaks.

It was on another journey with him through the entire backbone of the Canadian Rockies that a frying pan had somehow been omitted from the food chest. King had a brand new shovel. He cleaned this by shoving it into the shore sand several times, then washing off all the grit in the mountain brook beside which we'd camped the night before. With its large flat surface and long handle, it made an ideal utensil for frying the bacon and eggs with which it was soon sizzling.

Another time in that section of the river system, precisely at the tiny trading settlement of Finlay Forks, the individual who was handling the two-way radio there wanted someone to take his place long enough to allow him to go out to Prince George to be married. Roy Sharpe, the operator, made contact with King through telegrapher Fred Gaylor at Hudson Hope. Gaylor had bought the shortwave set of Dave Cuthill, a Scot who was managing the newly built Hudson's Bay Company buildings. King amiably agreed to boat up and fill in.

At the creek known as Six Mile, which was that far west of the Portage, he found Billy Kruger and Ed and Louis Stranberg building a shortwave radio. True to his nature, King tarried to help. The assistance eventually turned into a matter of days, and by the time King had the set functioning, he listened in on a conversation from the worrying Ray Sharpe, anxious about his impending wedding.

"They were talking about my shortcomings," King said afterward, "or maybe I'd better say, late-comings. I remember saying, 'By Jove, fellows, I guess I'd better start right out and travel all night. It's one thing to be late with the mail. But, I shouldn't make a man late for his own wedding!' "

Typically, he waved aside all thanks and didn't even bother to say good-bye.

King really didn't have the original contract to take the mail from Hudson Hope to Finlay Forks and Fort Graham. What King eventually got was a renewal of his brother Wesley's mail contract at 150 dollars a month. King was only fourteen years old when he first made the 350-mile round trip, with many stops along the way where trappers and prospectors were camped.

The regular contract was for travel by boat from May

through October. It also involved two cold-weather trips over-land or on the river when the ice was solid enough. Then the mailman had to backpack the first class mail, as well as his grub, blankets, and snowshoes. The wilderness postmen had many hazardous experiences. During Wes Gething's later trips he brought King along until, finally, King took over the run himself.

Geologists speak of the Gething Strata—mostly coal with some shale, conglomerate, and sandstone—named after King's father and running through the Hudson Hope area to the foothills near Calgary.

But Dr. F. H. McLearn has named an unusual starfish fossil *Kingii*. I have a number of specimens of this, found by Vena and myself a mile above Box Canyon by Deep Creek, which I have since called Starfish Creek. One on my desk is composed of layer after layer of shale, each with its perfectly formed tiny golden specks, just like the stars some children used to collect on their Sunday school attendance records.

Another fossil named after King is the shell of a small prehistoric creature which crawled on its stomach and small feet, the *Kingi Gethingi Gastropod*. There is another fossil called *Sagenites Gethingi*.

It took a lot to impress King. Once he and his youngest brother and fellow prospector Lloyd were visiting us in California, when we were temporarily Outside while I was doing some research. Vena and I took them on a special tour of the famous Hearst Castle at San Simeon, a gift to the State into which the late publisher William Randolph Hearst had poured a million dollars a year for fifty years on art alone, much of it becoming integral parts of the mountaintop edifice.

In his quiet way King was enraptured with everything, and we wondered what his final comment would be.

It was, "By Jove, what do they do with the garbage?"

King was soon back in his beloved Far North, cruising the upper Peace River where, no matter how hurried and harried his passengers might be, his philosophy was, "Another dry tree, another kettle of tea."

12

Sourdough Hercules

▲

WYNDHAM SCOTTY SMITH, a miner at King Gething's coal workings, was the strongest man Vena and I have ever known. When we first saw him, he was one of five men who were carrying a heavy motor from King's blacksmith shop where that master-of-all-trades had been welding a gear. Four truck drivers and miners were managing the rear of the machine, two on each side of a long crowbar thrust through its innards. Scotty by himself was carrying the front.

A remittance man from Scotland, Scotty had attended the University of Edinburgh and was the youngest son of a family who owned a thriving pub. His weakness was liquor, and his despairing relations finally shipped him off to Canada.

"When the ship got into Montreal, the first billboard I saw read, 'Drink Canada Dry,'" Scotty often said. "I've been trying to do that ever since."

Massive although not more than six feet tall, he had the short, straight, uncombed hair of a monk and a ruddy, clean-cut, open face, with a pair of wide-set eyes of the blueness you saw in the clear western sky during a chinook. The only demeaning part of his visage was the result of a drunken spree with a dentist in Alberta, during which the latter pulled all his teeth.

He had false teeth that, unfortunately, did not fit, although he sometimes wedged them in place with bits of coal. Because of his almost perpetual merriness you soon forgot this shortcoming, and with just his hard gums he managed to put away vast quantities of game meat, his favorite food. Scotty had great shoulders and a mighty chest, with arms whose bulging muscles showed to advantage when, the better to work, he stripped the upper part of his body to the long-handled underwear he always wore.

Scotty was far from being a constant tippler. He went for months without a drink, saving his wages with such penuriousness that he once bought two left shoes because, although they made his feet sore, they were cheaper. He wore clothing from surplus stores, letting his money accumulate under King Gething's protection until he had amassed the some two thousand dollars that bespoke another celebration.

Vena and I often occupied one of a line of small cottages at King's second mine. Scotty himself, prospecting with the rest of the crew, had discovered the eight-and-one-half-foot seam. We enjoyed King's interesting, easy-going hospitality in those days of relaxed game laws. Although never a thing was ever asked of us, I helped pay our way by hunting moose, bear, and deer for the long table.

In fact, when he saw us arriving again, Scotty invariably let out a whoop of delight, for he knew that savory steaks and sizzling roasts would soon be forthcoming. This was especially true when Charlie and Kay Ohland were working there, with neat, chubby as well as pretty Kay serving as cook.

Scotty was ever ready to help bring in the meat. This was always an occasion of merriment, for although he could shoulder the average mule deer and smaller black bear with ease, Scotty suffered some of the disadvantages of being musclebound. His feet could not avoid the frequent obstacles. He was always falling with a flurry of oaths. Scotty was good-natured about it all, which was just as well, for it was a constant source of uncontrollable hilarity when, with Wyndham Smith bearing the heaviest part of the load, he'd stumble over a deadfall and crash down anew with a flood of sincere but jocund curses.

I remember the evening when, after a day of tracking, I downed by far the two largest mule bucks I have ever seen. They were at their fattest, too, for it was just before the rut. Charlie Ohland, a former Swedish sailor and ship's carpenter who had cruised all over the world before settling down as a naturalized Canadian, eligible to homestead and work, borrowed a rope and single pulley. The two of us went across the steeply sloping, burned, northern face of Bullhead to hoist the choice meat to where the bears were not so likely to get at it before we had an opportunity to bring it in.

Those bucks were so massive that, although we cut the larger of them in two, we could not hoist the lower half more than a few feet off the ground even with the help of the well-oiled pulley, certainly not out of the danger zone. Charlie had the thick arms and wrists of a seafarer, too, and I was in top condition.

So King, Scotty, Charlie, Colin Campbell who was in for a truckload of coal, Bud Lawrence who drove Colin's second truck, and I elected to go out that evening to pack in as much venison as we could carry. The whole camp was meat hungry and was encouraged by a feast of the fresh liver I had brought back with me that twilight.

We carried what packs there were, I a Trapper Nelson type of packboard built by Bill Carter. Scotty who, even when he was unloaded, seemed unable to pick up his feet or to keep his balance, had a hard time following me through the mile-and-a-half of brule. Every time he fell it was with a thump and a storm of heartfelt curses at his own clumsiness.

We each shouldered as much as we could carry, intending to go back the next morning for the remainder. Scotty naturally bore the heaviest part. The lingering Northern dusk gave way to moonlight before we returned, and Scotty, who could not find his way alone through the wilderness, followed behind with Charlie. The going, if open, was steep and uncommonly rough. Every now and then I, in the lead, heard a fresh breaking of the burned downfall and another burst of bewailing.

Scotty, when he finally reached the cookshack, joined us in the outburst at the ludicrous figure he cut. Although he was unhurt except for the odd scrape and bruise, the exhausted Scot was a bundle of rags. But he was happy because he could visualize the banquets to follow. That night King got on his shortwave radio to Ted Vince in Fort St. John, whose lights we could see 70 miles to the east, and ordered a new set of inexpensive work clothes for Scotty, to be brought in by Milton Vince with the next truck.

Nor was this the only such episode. Scotty loved wild meat so much that he was always the first volunteer to assist in bringing in game, and there was always the same stumbling, falling, and streams of curses.

For the greater part of the year Scotty was a sober, hardworking man, a merry and brilliant conversationalist, who bettered the majority of his evenings listening to the news on a radio King had built for me in a dynamite box, and thoughtfully playing cribbage with Vena, using one of Bill Carter's homemade cribbage boards and pegs.

"You should go to Mexico sometime, Scotty," Vena and I kept telling him. "There you can get a quart of Bacardi rum for a dollar, and you would be seeing new country."

Scotty always enthusiastically agreed, and once we even had a flight to Mexico City booked for him. But when he picked up his two thousand dollars or so and set off with the best of intentions on another hard-earned vacation, he never got further than the Pomeroy Hotel in Fort St. John.

He was ever the convivial host, and when Hudson Hope finally got a beer parlor of its own in an appendage to the little log hotel, that kept him nearer home. The evening when Vena and I with Kay Ohland drank beer with him at one of the tables and insisted on catching every other check was, as far as I know, the first time that anyone managed to pay his own way on one of Scotty's toots.

The Hudson Hope Hotel would have no drinking in its rooms, so in town Scotty often stayed with Art Pollon and filled the latter's single-room cabin, on Mel Kyllo's property across from the Gethings, with cases of beer, rum, and whiskey. Everyone was welcome, and Scotty never lacked for fellow revelers. The only time I ever heard that he became angry was when he caught an Indian sneaking out with an armload of Canadian Club fifths.

Generous though Scotty was, he would scarcely pay a penny for his own well-being. He kept his parties going days and nights until his last cent and his credit were exhausted. Then, sick and gaunt, for he never tempered his imbibing with eating, he'd wait for King to load him into his truck and take him back up the mountain for another stint of the hardest of labor and self-enforced economy.

He was early obsessed with the not-unhappy belief that he would die by forty, and so he never saw any need for saving money. He was pleasantly amazed when he approached the age of fifty.

It all came to an end one evening when Scotty, working the new mine alone, did not walk back the half-mile for supper. King, investigating the tunnels with his hard miner's hat with its attached battery-powered light, found Scotty dead of a heart attack below an unfinished hole he had been boring for a dynamite charge.

Wyndham Smith was a sourdough Hercules, a scholar, a gourmand, an understanding listener, a fine friend, and a gentleman.

Fall mist rising from the Peace River in early morning. The old-timers say the haze is composed of the ghosts of departed sourdoughs.

Rocky Mountain Canyon.   **The view upriver from our cabin.**

Vena by our Peace River cabin.

Dudley "Deadly" Shaw, sourdough *par excellence*.

Jean Gething. You couldn't ask for a better wilderness neighbor.

Outfitter Gary Powell with a wild Canada Jay eating from his hand.

Lily, former chief of the Beaver Indians on the headwaters of the Graham River north of Hudson Hope. The Graham is part of the Halfway River system which flows into the Peace.

An Indian cache further north. Joe Barkley is about to ford a river. "This deep?" he's asking. The Indian nods in agreement. In just three steps Joe and his horse were in over their heads and swimming for it.

Joe Barkley, a few years later, returning from his trap line with Lupe, an Airedale, and Buster, a husky.

Gary Powell with his pack string in the mountains north of Hudson Hope.

Olive Beattie Powell. If you've never eaten bear stew, your life is poorer for it.

Elizabeth Beattie and Kay Ohland near our cabin.

Vena watering our horses, Cloud and Chinook, in front of our cabin.

Claire and Joe Barkley before their marriage. The license plate reads "ALBERTA 1926."

The Barkleys now, in front of their cabin.

| *13* |

Buds Bursting Like Popcorn

▲

SPRING SOMETIMES arrived unannounced, a prolonged chinook just blowing along until you suddenly realized the new season had come. In any event, it is always exciting to be standing amid poplars on a balmy April morning and listening to the leaf buds burst open with the ardor of popping corn.

The crusted snow now settled in swishing sections well ahead of our boots as we walked through the deeper forest. Snowbanks smoked, and the melting woods were alive with the music of countless streamlets whose arteries surged with the ebbing vitality of winter. There was a warm earthy pungency to everything. Across the river, around the thawing beaver meadow, the soft light green of the hardwoods began to manifest itself like an accumulating cloud.

It's always a dramatic event when the ice goes out. Overflow first cut channels in the thick covering, surging in ever broadening streams over the still frozen highway. Ice finally split, severed, and eventually shattered into jumbled cakes. White masses of slush frosted the spaces between. Then parts of the gelid Peace River started to break free until finally, perhaps at sunrise, grating, crashing cakes jumbled together in a gigantic golden trough.

Soon the flood shrank, stranding blocks as high and wide as cottages on the cluttered shore. By the time we'd begin to think that these would have to melt away under the increasing stress of the smoldering sun, the river would once again rise, sweeping everything along with it including shore-stranded driftwood and live trees whose roots revolved burdensomely and luringly in the flood. Clamorous wild geese, swans, ducks, and sandhill cranes winged on their way above the somehow orderly chaos, turning northward in the Continental Trough. Some great Canada geese always tarried to nest in the islands opposite our cabin.

I came upon King Gething one day when I rode toward his sister Vesta's for the weekly mail. Shambling toward the H.B.C., his long intelligent face sober, he stopped to talk. His dark brown eyes seemed deeper than I had ever seen them. He was tall and lank, carelessly clothed and somewhat bent, like a scholar. The roughness of his face, unshaven for several days, made stronger the boniness of his countenance.

He'd early begun mining coal on his own Crown lease on the northeastern side of Bullhead, in a minor canyon through which twinkled a stream from a muskeg and spring higher up the slope. King's mine was the first after the grant-proving Gething-Aylard-Green riverside tunnel. Dominating it was a high wide trestle, on which the machine shop, the narrow car-bearing tracks, and truck-loading hopper depended.

"To operate a coal mine in the wilderness," King had told me once, "you don't exactly have to be a combination prospector, miner, surveyor, logger, sawmill expert, blacksmith, welder, backwoodsman, road builder, contractor, all-around engineer, freighter, accountant, cook, and natural manager. But it helps."

"The bear are sure enough raising aitch up at my mine," King said that morning, his hand touching the butt of my rifle that slanted under my right knee in a hand-tooled scabbard. "You'd certainly be doing me a favor if you rode up and dispatched a few of them before they entirely wreck the cookshack. I'll be along with Bill Currie in my pickup in a few days to see about opening for the spring. Neither of us is much of a shot, though, and the disturbance we'll make is apt to keep away the prime offenders, anyway. There's oat bundles there for your horse Chinook, and it's warm enough so that your saddle blanket will be plenty at night. Some grub's around if the bears haven't got it all."

"Glad to," I agreed after a moment of thought. "I'll go right now if you'll take the mail and some Canada bacon I've ordered at the Bay up to Vena and let her know where I'll be the next couple of days."

"Consider it done," King said, and as he turned he raised his long-fingered hand in a gesture of farewell.

The signs of the bears' ravages were all around even before I rode up the final twist of road. A blanched white line from a torn flour sack streaked the trail before vanishing into the heavy second growth. I tethered Chinook under a semblance of roof, gave her a sheaf of oats, then walked the remaining seventy odd yards.

The cookhouse was a shambles. Bears, hungry from their winter's sleep—not hibernation, for bears do not actually hibernate—had been lured by the clinging odors of last season's sizzling bacon and plopping hotcakes. The bears had been everywhere. Stretches of asphalt-impregnated roofing paper had been ripped away. That the door had been smashed in was to be expected, but the bruins had even clawed off the planks left spiked over the two broad windows and entered through the broken sashes.

There were even flour-white paw marks along the top of the large iron cookstove. What the animals had not devoured was pretty much destroyed. Several remaining cans of beans and other vegetables had been punctured by keen fangs and their contents left to rot. That the situation was crucial was apparent, because I knew that the expenses of constructing and operating the mine were at best scarcely more than covered by the intake.

The truckers distributing the coal—including friends like Colin Campbell, Ray Fells, Les Bazeley, Bud Lawrence, Ted and Milton Vince, and several others who helped King maintain his road and who were given preferential treatment in return—pocketed the greater proportion of the gross. Something had to be done, and soon.

I didn't want to make my presence known. So during my lone stay there I ate raw potatoes from a sack still remaining in the cold cellar. The water from the spring was cold and refreshing. I chose my observation point near the cabins. It was a high platform which was spiked among four large and trimmed poplars whose trunks had been sheathed with discarded stovepipe and with flattened cans to frustrate clawed climbers. Instead of watching and listening for intruders, I kept my eyes on Chinook.

That the bears, a notably nonsocial species, had been foraging in shifts soon became evident. The first bruin appeared below at about four o'clock. I dispatched him with a single head shot halfway between eye and ear and climbed down the ladder which I had moved into place. With my rifle still ready, I dressed him out and suspended him with a rope around his neck, to drain from a pole already stretched between two high poplar branches in front of the guest cabin. Then I returned to my seat.

Nothing happened during the moonlit night, although I slept lightly. The next bear showed up at six o'clock in the morning. I got that one with a single shot, too, which was fortunate for my supply of cartridges was limited. I dressed it out but, because my lariat was already in use, settled for laying it opened, its middle downward, across some poles under which there was ample ventilation. Then I had another feed of raw potatoes and replenished my canteen. There was a third bear to be dealt with at four in the afternoon.

That night, apprehensive lest some bear had waddled past me the night before in the dimness, I renailed planks across the broken windows, fixed and bolted the door, moved the mattress from a corner cot to the long and wide table in the middle of the single room, and went to sleep with flashlight and rifle beside me. Nothing happened, but at six o'clock in the morning when I was walking up the hill after watering and feeding Chinook, the largest bear of them all appeared at the upper edge of the clearing.

It was a fairly long shot, so I lay down and aimed for the middle of the shoulder so as to anchor the animal if I did not kill it outright. As it happened, the bullet split upon contact, part of it piercing the heart.

That was the end of that adventure, and when King and Bill Currie drove up about ten o'clock, King asked if anything had happened. I led him around to the back of the building to see the quartet that had evidently been doing the most damage. It was the only time I ever saw King aghast. Silently he extended his right hand for me to shake.

Then, raising his voice, something which was also very unusual for him, he called, "By Jove, Bill! Come back here and have a look!"

Although King did not get back to the mine permanently until midsummer to complete repairs, replenish his supplies, replace several stretches of corduroy on the road, and start filling his hoppers with coal once again, there was no more bear damage; not, at least, for that year.

King was much like an absent-minded college professor, highly intellectual, always pondering, and oblivious to many minor things of the moment. Once when Vena was visiting back in Boston, I was staying with him at the mine, hunting for camp meat as usual. On one occasion King made a point of inviting me to town with him where he was screening a movie that night. I accepted and started to get ready. It was not until some time later that I realized King had driven away alone.

"How's Brad?" his father asked him when he reached home.

King looked blank for a moment. Then he said, "By Jove, I was supposed to bring him with me."

He was all apologetic when he returned the next morning.

Another time when Vena, King, and I were the only occupants at the camp, he invited us to have tea with him after supper in the cookshack. At the same time he challenged Vena to play him for the constantly changing cribbage championship.

"Let me take some of this hot water first," he said "and I'll go down to my cabin and shave."

We waited fifteen minutes, twenty minutes, and finally half an hour. Then we thought to look through the doorway at King's window. The lights were all out. He had forgotten and gone to sleep.

Riding with him in his truck was always an experience. The continuation of the road to the new mine was normally deserted, and when King had to turn around on it to return to camp, which he'd located by a large spring a half mile from the vein, he never looked to see where he was backing. This made good enough sense when one stopped to think about it, for the road was narrow, and there was nothing on either side but poplars. But it was disconcerting at first to sit in the front seat while King backed, without a glance behind him, until he hit a barrier and then, changing gears, completed the turn.

Once when Vena and I were staying at the mine without our horses, we elected on an especially magnificent morning to take lunches and a tea pail, descend to the river, and hike along the bank to town. Our plan was to return later with King, who was leaving that day for some business in Fort St. John; we'd spend the intervening several days with friends. To lighten our packs, King promised to bring our duffle bag of personal belongings to town and leave it with his father, Vesta, and brother Larry, later a town councilman.

Needless to say, King forgot to take the duffle bag out of the truck, and we had to pick up toothbrushes and several other necessities at the Bay. Impishly, Vena made King pay for her toothbrush, which *fine* he accepted with an apologetic grin.

It was when he was on the Peace that one could see how he had won his cognomen "King of the River." We made several trips with him in my little Douglas plywood 13-footer, named by Vena the *Peacemaker,* up the lower half of Rocky Mountain Canyon to the old mine. It was he who taught me the channels.

After the bear episode, Vena and I were soon together again, watching the spring flood bringing the water level completely over the river edge to the foot of our lane. We took our empty buckets to it every day. No faucets? No trouble with plumbing and water rationing! No electricity? No utility bills!

As the growth greened like spring fire, we lived more and more off the country. It was only natural. Long before the human race thought of raising them in gardens and on ranches and farms, all our basic fruits and vegetables grew wild. They still do, of course, and now they nourished us bountifully.

What pastime can furnish the same amount of pure and vital pleasure, with so little outlay and with such delectable returns, as the gathering of edible wild plants? As we became more and more interested and knowledgeable, each stroll in the wilds about our home was changed from a pleasurable hike to an eager and rewarding quest. Each walk became an opportunity for becoming acquainted with new natural edibles and for enjoying purposeful hours of exhilarating and rewarding excitement.

It was putting into action the natural yearning of that portion of our most primitive ancestor which survives in each of us. Most people fret that if forced to shift for themselves away from stores, they would famish. Yet there are actual forests of food.

We tapped the birches about our woodland home each spring as if they were maples, boiling down the sap and then spreading it over our sourdough pancakes. We ate the brittle tips of the new blue spruce and lodgepole pine sprigs, then brewed tea from them that tasted Christmasy. Arctic expert Vilhjalmur Stefansson, now "Stef" to us, wrote us how the early Jacques Cartier exploration party was saved from scurvy that had already developed among them by such an evergreen brew.

Neil and Vesta Gething were always pointing out some new wild edible to us, and the trappers and prospectors like Dudley Shaw and Bill Carter each had their own favorites. It was Dick Hamilton, for instance, who showed us that the nettle which nearly everyone avoids because of its prickles and which has to be gathered with gloves and a knife and bag, loses its formidableness as soon as the dark emerald plants are dropped into boiling water. Almost instantly ready for serving with a pat of margarine or butter, it is one of North America's more delicious greens.

It really isn't necessary to become accustomed to wild potherbs, as they are like familiar acquaintances. Many of them are not only similar to the vegetables retailed in markets, but they frequently excel them in flavor and in usages. The common pigweed, for instance, can not only be eaten like spinach, having a more subtle taste than that common green, but its seeds can become cereal.

Salsify and silverweed both remind one of parsnips in flavor, and both of them can be employed in numerous ways in which parsnips are not generally enjoyed. Knotweed and young milkweed can be handled like asparagus, several changes of water being used in the preparation of the latter, and they have a savor all their own. One species of knotweed can even be readied like rhubarb, the leaves of which domestic plant happen to be poisonous. Whether these potherbs are served plain, creamed, or just dropped into soups and casseroles, they provide some of the tastier eating known to man. It's like springtime on the stove.

Yellow jackets, not troubling us as we walked past them, cheerily buzzed the flowering pussy willows that soon were everywhere. Finches, the familiar robins, redwing blackbirds with their bright little chevrons on each wing, and the first of the coming cliff swallows added to the general exhilaration. The smallest of blue moths brushed us. The ground itself had an earthy and promising aroma.

On the other side of the Peace, mists of light green clung to the tops of the tall poplars. This haze became brighter and thicker. Finally the week was reached when Vena and I could no longer glimpse the forest floor beneath or even the single branches.

"Insofar as vegetation is involved," King told us one morning, "each 1,000 feet you gain in elevation is the same as journeying 600 miles deeper into the north. And that far from here would put us up by Great Bear Lake in the Northwest Territories, close to the still frozen Arctic Ocean."

"That's right," Neil added. "On the plains, as you know, spring travels north about fifteen miles a day. When you reach a mountain like these here, it climbs about 600 feet a week."

So that's why we rode up to Beryl Prairie and Chinaman Lake, to catch up with the vanishing winter.

| *14* |

Recapturing Winter

▲

ON BERYL PRAIRIE we hastened past Joe and Claire Barkley's, then Dennis and Jessie Murphy's, promising at both places to stop on the way back. Spring fever was in our blood, but as we gained elevation when we swung west toward the Butler Range, a straight snow-topped arrow pointing north, the unshod hooves of our horses Chinook and Cloud began crunching through portions of muskeg which were still brittle with ice.

The ground was becoming generally brown and bare at these altitudes in contrast to the green around our cabin. Drifts of snow were vaporizing in the brilliant sunshine whose warmth, tempered by wind brisk from dazzling mountains just before our eyes, felt pleasant about us at these colder heights. More and more, the white mounds lay deeper and closer to one another. We rode to the top of another ridge, on which was a fallen-in cabin. Straight ahead was the small face of Chinaman Lake.

"Look," Vena said. "It hasn't thawed yet."

Luckily for the horses, grass had begun to green among the remainders of coarse, granular snow. Picketing Chinook and Cloud on long lariats, the end of each attached to a lower foreleg with a nonjamming and nonslipping bowline knot, we spread nearby our air mattresses and mummy bags. These had been rolled, our rations and limited duffle inside, and tied behind the cantles of our saddles.

Wolf tracks were everywhere. In one area of the mountainside along the western shore of the lake, where the snow was packed as solidly as a miniature skating rink, there were the recently stripped skeletons of two moose. The sight made our hearts beat faster.

"There isn't the slightest possibility of their troubling us," I reassured Vena, "but we'd better tie Bushman by us at night. It's a favorite trick of a pack to lure even as large a dog as an Irish wolfhound into the woods with one lone wolf, then for the entire pack to attack and eat him."

"He seems to realize the danger instinctively, doesn't he?" Vena said. "Still, I'll sleep a lot better with him on a leash. But see how close he's been staying ever since we've arrived here. And he'll chase coyotes without a single thought."

We slumbered under the stars that night, with a campfire comradely burning and the shadowy shapes of the two horses and Bushman vague in its far-reaching flicker of flames.

"Aw-wa-oooo-ooh." The nearby howl of a timber wolf, blood-quickening under the moon, woke us up sometime during the darkness. Reaching out a hand, I could feel Bushman in a trembling coil by my head. A wolf sounds different when you're camping alone, the only humans within miles. "Aw-wa-ooooooooo."

We drifted back to sleep. Instantly, it was morning.

We stayed three days there at Chinaman Lake, living mainly off the country, on varying hare which were everywhere that year, on edible wild plants and berries, and on the fatly succulent and nourishing marrow we got by roasting the larger bones of the two freshly killed moose, then cracking them open with rocks.

Winter left us quickly when we descended to the flatness of Beryl Prairie. Dennis and Jessie were away somewhere. It was spring again when we reached the low hominess of the Barkley cabin. Claire showed us the tops of radishes already coming up in her fenced garden, next to the large barn and adjoining corral. Hungry for companionship, we all talked far into the night before Claire brewed a final pot of Fort York tea from the H.B.C., and Vena and I, sated and happy, retired to the spare bedroom.

Clara, who likes our calling her Claire, and Joe Barkley, who won't answer to his real first name, told us of their early days on Beryl Prairie. They had been among the first settlers on this level expanse of fertile land, a few miles northwest of Hudson Hope. With King Gething's mine road only a few yards further along the Portage to the left, there is a slight incline down to the plain which, because of fires and clearing, is now largely well-advanced second growth. One really has to hunt on horseback to see over it.

Both Joe and Claire were born in Alberta in 1908.

"In those days," Joe told us, and he wrinkled his strong long nose that jutted between the two sharp blue eyes, "her folks were considered well-to-do. I had nothing."

Both are slim and trim even now. Working side by side as they always have in the expanding oat fields and the garden of their homestead, which they soon proved up and began to increase, neither had put on any weight. Joe is of lank, medium height and has a spare, thoughtful face. Claire, with a deft hand, was pushing a strand of graying brown hair, darker than Joe's, out of her soft hazel eyes and away from the fragrant steam of a bubbling mulligan stew.

She was roofing this with dumplings. It seethed on the polished black top of her wood-burning stove. Both Vena and I leaned forward interestedly, as it is not for nothing that Claire is noted for being the best cook on Beryl Prairie.

"I'll never forget how Joe and I met at a dance in Alberta in 1928," Claire told us, and her sudden flush seemed not entirely from the warmth of the cooking. "The first year went along smoothly. Then when Dad thought that things were becoming serious, he began objecting."

"In 1930," Joe remembered with a grin, "I asked permission to marry her. He told me to get off the place and stay off. I said, 'Fine, but I'll be back to get her.' "

He reached up a calloused hand from where he was shaving fuzzsticks, for starting the cooking fire the next morning, and gave Claire's arm an affectionate squeeze.

"That's when I left for the Peace River country," Joe told us. "My brother, Larnie, came with me. At that time there was no work to be found in our part of Alberta or anywhere close by. An old gentleman told me that if he were a young man, he'd head for Hudson Hope. So that's what we did.

"In 1930 the end of the steel was at Hythe, Alberta, 170 miles from Hudson Hope. We caught a ride to Dawson Creek in the mail truck. From there we rode with another mail carrier to Fort St. John, where we stayed overnight. We came up the Peace River from Taylor Flats with Pat Callison in the mail boat, a two-day trip.

"From Hudson Hope we walked out to Beryl Prairie, to the cabin of Herb Coulson. Herb, who you remember spent the summer with us not too long ago, was to become one of our neighbors. We stayed overnight with him. He fed us some bear meat which he had canned and which we thought was as delicious as beef. We were nearly starving."

It's a funny thing about bear meat. When I was writing a book on survival, I tasted every kind of wild meat I could come by handily—wolf, lynx, coyote, beaver, muskrat, squirrel, varying hare, game birds, an Indian-killed swan, and so on, together with moose, caribou, antelope, deer, and the like. I also sampled opinions. Those who dine on black bear fairly often, I found, are almost unanimously agreed that the North American wilderness affords no more delectable game meat with the single exception of young mountain sheep. And this last is the best meat, wild or tame, I've ever relished anywhere.

Many hunters, most of them who've never tasted bear meat nor smelled it cooking, are prejudiced against the omnivore as food for some reason or another. For one thing, when skinned whole a bear superficially resembles a man. Another cause often heard has to do with the animal's eating habits, although the most ravenous bear is a finicky diner when compared to a lobster or a chicken, and most people think the latter two taste just fine.

It's true that not even a plump young yearling furnishes good steaks, which is where many culinary efforts conclude. The meat has to be broiled so long that it becomes tough and stringy. But even an oldster large enough to carpet a large cabin will cook up into such roasts and stews that you have to eat them to believe them. The meat then so resembles top-grade beef that you can serve it as such to individuals who've vowed they'd never touch bear meat and actually have them coming back for second and third helpings. All in all, if bear didn't provide such feasts, I would have given up hunting them long ago.

Any excess fat should be trimmed off before the meal is cooked. This fat should then be slowly heated in open pans to extract the grease. Strained into jars, that of the black bear hardens into a clear white lard that any user, including Claire, considers the best she has ever tried. That procured from a grizzly remains a more easily measured oil. Both are esteemed in the Farther Places for everything from medicine to mixing with molasses for Yankee Butter.

"That year," Joe continued, "I worked in a road camp, and in the fall I went home. In the spring of 1931, a friend and my two brothers left Camrose with me in a Model T Ford to drive as close as we could to Hudson Hope. Was that ever an experience!

"At Donvegan there was a foot of water on the Peace River ice. A fellow told us that every year someone went through the ice. He allowed that we just might make it, and then again we might be the ones to go through. Well, we made it."

At the Halfway, a usually small river half the distance between Fort St. John and Hudson Hope, they traded the Model
T for two horses, unbroken colts to be exact. The deal was
consummated with Joe's later very good friend, Phil Tompkins,
a dynamic sourdough who with his family was building a wilderness empire.

"My oldest brother and the friend who had come with us
stayed at the Halfway, and Larnie and I continued through to
the Hope. Larnie went to work at Joe Turner's, just outside the
town to the north-northeast. I hired on, below the Portage road
on Beryl Prairie, at the sawmill. This belonged entirely to
Wesley and Jean Gething. Wesley was the oldest son of the coal
mining family, and this Prairie happened to have been named
by an outsider after their pretty little daughter Beryl.

"The sawmill was three miles from my homestead here," Joe
went on, "so it was convenient for me to work on my cabin. I
worked at both places that summer. Bill Carter, Matt Boe, Earl
Pollon, and others were hired, along with me, to help move the
mill machinery from Brenham Flat to Beryl Prairie.

"Jean Gething cooked for about a dozen men while her husband ran the sawmill. Little Beryl was about five years old at
that time, and that was one of the only two years that Jean
didn't teach school. I worked there all summer, in my odd hours
trying to prove up this homestead. Then I had a personal fire,
due to my own negligence, and burned everything including my
wages. All I had left was the patched overalls I was wearing,
plus a quarter and a dime which I gave to Beryl. I went home
that fall, anyway, to marry my Clara."

Claire raised her bright eyes to Vena's and mine. "We eloped,"
she said, and somehow her hand and Joe's found one another,
while Vena's slim fingers squeezed mine.

"I'll never forget the date. It was October 7, 1931," Joe said.
"She went into her clothes closet and down through a trapdoor,

which was a winter entrance to the cellar. Then she came up the outside stairway. We lost no time in making our escape. I was never so scared in my life, but everything has turned out very well indeed. Even my father-in-law admitted that years later.

"We were delayed over two months at the flooding and freezing Halfway River. Mr. and Mrs. Tompkins took us in, and we helped them every way we could." Knowing the Barkleys' reticence, we could appreciate that was a lot. "They were very good to us."

"On the day before Christmas 1931 we arrived at our new little cabin. We had some pork fat from Mrs. Tompkins, while my mother had packed several cans of precious butter for us to take north with the little we were carrying," Joe said.

"I'm telling you," Claire put in, "we didn't waste a tiny bit."

"On Christmas day Larnie and I went moose hunting," Joe continued, "and Clara spent the day browsing through the T. Eaton catalog. How broke were we? Well, we had no cash at all, and if my mother hadn't sent us a few things, we would have been in very dire straits indeed. It was a rabbit year, and thank God for rabbits. Moose were as scarce as hen's teeth."

Claire was dishing up the dinner, and the kitchen was filled with savory smells.

"Come and get it," Claire said with a smile, "or I'll throw it away."

She didn't have to throw anything away. She wasn't the best cook on Beryl Prairie for nothing, and wilderness living, by whetting keen appetites, makes everything taste better.

As for Beryl Prairie, Herb Coulson and his son Ralph, having arrived respectively in 1929 and the spring of 1930, were Joe's and Larnie's first neighbors when they reached there in early June of 1930.

Matt Boe and Andy Lindberg arrived later in the summer. Oscar Bolding came to the Prairie a few months afterwards. The

Barkleys' neighbor to the east, Andrew Lehne, and their neighbor to the south, Teddy Yates, came in October 1931. Joe and Claire Barkley were 23 years old when they reached Hudson Hope.

The trouble with Beryl Prairie was that most homesteaders found it was difficult to sink a well successfully. An exception was Herb Coulson who managed to find water at a shallow depth. Vena and I watched Art Pollon doing the digging and cribbing in Joe's and Claire's final attempt, and we helped Joe windlass up some of the dirt. They sank a hole four feet square. All the time cribbing, they went down 85 feet. From that level they continued another 50 feet with a six-inch auger. There was wet gravel where they had to quit. There was no means of getting oxygen down the hole except for the air that settled there naturally.

Dennis Murphy, who eventually married Claire's younger sister, the curly brown-haired Jessie, was in the country longer than his bride. He worked a while gold mining on Brenham Flat, as did many another young fellow. Dennis had been born in Osborne, Kansas. His father had passed away in Sioux City.

Jessie finally came to Beryl Prairie, as she told Vena and me, to "visit my sister Clara and to see this Dennis Murphy she had been talking about and find out what he was really like. I found out. We were married in 1939. It was rough going in the thirties, as you know. Although Dennis had a homestead on Lynx Creek, there was no house and no money to speak of."

It was at Lynx Creek, it so happened, that Joe and many of the other settlers on Beryl Prairie got their water, hauling it with horses in big, untopped, scrubbed oil and gasoline drums.

"Dennis, a bookworm interested in archaeology and genealogy, was working in the post office in Henry Stege's store when I met him. I'm sure that if it weren't for the Barkleys, we'd never have survived homesteading. They were wonderful to us, as were the Gethings, Ted Yates, and the Kyllos.

"Wesley and Jean Gething had a sawmill, and only through their generosity were we able to get lumber for the floor and such to enable us to finish our log cabin. I cooked in exchange. I was no cook, mind you, but the men put up with what food there was. My rhubarb pies were something else. I can still hear Larry Gething asking me if I crimped the rim of the crust with my teeth.

"The mosquitoes were so numerous that we had to have a smudge pail under the table to smoke them away. We slept under nets. Then on weekends we'd stroll over to Ted Yates' to sample what he called his 'keg water' and which was a potent brew. Dennis and I wondered sometimes if those red ants that showed up in our tumblers gave it that special kick.

"Then there were our berry-picking days when the raspberries, strawberries, saskatoons, and the low Christmas cranberries were very plentiful. Many times we would be picking saskatoons and chokecherries around the hills above Guy Robison's, the Ardills', Tompkins', or Les Bazeley's, and we would wind up being overnight guests. Their hospitality had no limit.

"The Kyllos were such fun, also. Clara or I would walk to a dance, or just go to town, and wind up at their home. It was on one of those walks that we passed a survey camp at Four Mile Creek on the Portage. As we came close, we could see a young man going from tree to tree, very much interested in their bark. We were curious and asked him what he was doing. We knew he was a university student.

"He said, 'I want to write a letter home on birch bark. Where do I find it, on a poplar or on one of these burned pines?'

"Then the fire came from Twelve Mile where it had been started to clear grazing land. We watched it for a week or two, coming over the mountains from Jim Beattie's, never dreaming it would burn our way. How wrong we were!

"Some eighteen or so neighbors came to start a fire guard between Barkleys' and us which they hoped would stop and burn itself out. How wrong they were, too! It got fanned out of control, keeping the others from coming to our rescue. They were trapped on the Barkleys' side. Dennis, I, and Ed Broulette fought the fire alone. Little bones and such of birds and animals fell from the air, covering our garden with white ashes. We carried buckets of water to pour over the shakes of our roof, but the heat was so terrific that it dried immediately.

"We had eight sled dogs tied up, horses in the corral, cattle in the barn, and our chickens in the hen house to keep them from the flames. We kept Leon, our new baby, in a crib in a shed out in a clearing where I had stored bread that I'd baked for the fire fighters we expected.

"Lynx Creek furnished plenty of water, especially a pool where the stream made a bend a few hundred yards behind the buildings, but there wasn't much we could do with it. In fact, we finally realized that we could do nothing. So we put the baby's clothes and other easy-to-move things into the shed and re-signed ourselves to our house and barn burning.

"We turned all our livestock loose so that they could fend for themselves. I remember the dogs racing to eat up all the bread. Panic began to overtake us, especially me.

"Then all of a sudden an American soldier, driving a jeep, burst through the fire. How I blessed that boy! He had volunteered to go see what had happened to us. He got the baby, me, and as many things as we could cram into the vehicle and turned back through the flames and smoke. Prongs of fire shot over the jeep, against the windshield, and over our heads, but he kept going.

"After about three-quarters of a mile we broke into a clearing that had already burned. Deer, moose, bear, rabbits, you name it, were all in small gatherings, so terrified that they were paying no attention to anything. We were safe, and we eventually came to Clara, Joe, and the others.

"That evening it rained, and Dennis and Ed joined us. The

crook in the creek and its canyon, turning the wind, was all that
saved our place and the forest about it which Dennis had stub-
bornly, and rightly as it turned out, refused to backfire. Again
neighbors came forward and gave us shelter."

All they could think of, the survivors told me, was Dante's
Inferno. After that, things settled back into their former pace,
and the spring greenery started shooting up almost at once
through the ashes.

The past hard winter seemed far away.

| *15* |

Another of the North's Greats

▲

ALWIN HOLLAND was Hudson Hope's first schoolmaster. His first classes were held in Doc Fredette's cabin until the new little log school could be finished. Alwin became a close friend of ours, visiting us frequently after we had purchased and rebuilt Dudley Shaw's cabin. This was side by side with his property in the Glen, where the Gething coal used to be brought by sleigh. Only the narrow Peace River Block line separated us.

King Gething, who was willed the Holland estate after that gentleman died at age 80, later gave the Glen to the town of Hudson Hope as the Alwin Holland Memorial Park. An all-weather gravel road to the Glen, enhanced on both sides by luxuriant growths of dandelions and raspberries, was put in by King's efforts.

A small, well-built, quiet, and unassuming scholar, Holland was a graduate of McGill University and of the British Columbia Normal School. He was a former college principal, an engineer, and a surveyor. We frequently encountered him in this last capacity, when he was surveying King Gething's coal holdings on Bullhead. He also surveyed the Halfway River Bridge, an important link between Hudson Hope and Fort St. John.

Born in Grey County, Ontario, Alwin put in a full career as a teacher and head of the Kamloops Presbyterian College and the Armstrong School. Alwin enlisted in 1914 with the Seventh

Battalion, 88th Regiment. He went with the Canadian forces to France where he was captured the next year in the second battle of Ypres. All in all, he served three years and seven months as a prisoner of war, undergoing particularly harsh treatment after an unsuccessful attempt to escape.

After demobilization he returned to the Peace River country in 1919, taking up land in Fort St. John where we sometimes had long talks with him over steaming cups of tea. The year after his army discharge, though, he journeyed to Victoria to continue his course in surveying, later became articled to the well-known Frank Swannel, and was finally certified. In later years gas and oil were discovered on his Fort St. John tract, but unfortunately the British Columbia Government had retained all mineral rights as has been their usual custom.

During 1921 Mr. Holland commenced Presbyterian mission work at Fort St. John and Taylor Flats. It was the following year that he opened the Hudson Hope elementary school where the young Gethings and MacDougalls were among his pupils. The next year he taught in Fort St. John. At the same time he was proving up his homestead.

Alwin had long admired the work of the Anglican missionaries, and so he donated the Fort St. John property now known as The Abbey to Monica Storrs, a frequent visitor to the area, and to the Fellowship of the West which sponsored her religious work in our part of the country.

He opened the Attachie School at the Halfway in 1926, the Rose Prairie School in 1930, and the Bear Flat School during the following year.

During World War II he was called upon by the Canadian Government and the Department of Transport to locate airports along the Northwest Staging Route. He was in charge of the Watson Lake installation up the Alaska Highway until paving started there, then went on to survey at Teslin, icy Snag, and the Wolf Lake Weather Station.

Afterwards he returned to teaching in Hudson Hope for a while, assisted Duncan Cran with land surveying in the area, opened the Moose Creek School, and did some substituting at Upper Cache Creek. It was only fitting that after the oil and gas boom in Fort St. John, the new elementary school in the Pacific subdivision there was named in his honor.

"He was a well-loved teacher, surveyor, and friend," Jean Gething told me during the writing of this book. "An invitation was sent to him for the testimonial dinner the school board gave me. He came to Dawson Creek from Fort St. John for it. It was a real effort, and I felt very honored. But when he was asked to speak, he had to refuse since his voice was so unsteady."

16

Shivaree

▲

JEAN VICTORIA MCLARTY went to school with some of the Gethings in Prince George. The Gething children were Wesley, Larry, Lillian, King, Vesta, and Lloyd, all to be prominent in Hudson Hope history. When Jean met Wesley in Giscome, about 20 miles east of Prince George where she had gone to teach and where he had a railway-tie contract, they started going together. The next Easter they were married in Prince George.

When school was out, after Wes had put in the cool spring prospecting and fur trading, they met at Peace River Crossing and had a summer of honeymooning on the Peace River. Their first trip was on the freight and passenger boat *Lady Jane,* dubbed *"Lazy"* by the sourdoughs because it took so long to get anywhere. They were a week in reaching Hudson Hope since the craft stopped to load lumber at Taylor Flats and make other frequent stops.

"Our first night in Hudson Hope, there was a dance, of course," Jean told me, "and about midnight Wesley asked me to meet him outside the school where the affair was being held. He took me for a long walk by a roundabout way until I suddenly discovered that he had cannily arranged a bed and blankets in some remote willows. This is where we spent our first night.

"We had been there only about an hour when we heard drums beating, tin cans rattling, horns blaring, and bells ringing. We finally realized that the town was mistakenly shivareeing the tent where Wesley's two sisters, Vesta and Lillian, were staying. Wesley says I got up, clasped my arms around a stump, and said, 'Home, sweet home.' This was our shivaree.

"Later a friend from California took us on a trip aboard the big riverboat, the *D. A. Thomas,* to Peace River Crossing. The *D. A. Thomas* was a beautiful stern-wheeler. It had quite a few staterooms and a lovely dining room and ballroom. Most of the sourdoughs had a dinner and dance on it whenever it came to town. In the remote wilderness especially, it was like going to a hotel.

"We voyaged back on Captain Harry Weaver's *Lady Jane* where we were supposed to occupy a tent on a scow. There turned out to be some cheechako teachers on the trip, though, and they had to share the tent with me. So Wesley and I didn't get together again until we reached Rolla Landing. On the way upriver the girls tried to help cook meals and take care of things, but they didn't know much about roughing it. Wesley and I took over the cooking.

"Wesley was bowman for the boat, which had an inboard motor, and every once in a while he'd wave to some man on shore and shout, 'Hi, Al.' One of the young teachers finally asked me why everyone was called Al around here?

"Wesley answered, 'Well, there was an old Pap Al up in this country. He had a squaw in every camp, so he called all his boys 'Al.'

"Later we put in at Rolla Landing, and the man who came to meet the boat was game warden Van Dyke. Wesley stepped off the gangplank and said jovially, 'Well, if it isn't old Pap Al himself.' Of course, the impressionable girls thought there really was a relationship, but I don't think the game warden ever knew what had happened.

"The next morning Captain Harry Weaver gave Wesley and

me breakfast in bed, in what was now our own tent in the bow of the scow, to make up for all the time we had been cooking for the gang."

The hazards always looming in the Farther Places were emphasized by the drowning of Bob Porter while ascending the treacherous Black Canyon on the Omineca River. Here the Omineca narrowed some dozen miles from where the stream met the Finlay River, about 25 miles up from Finlay Forks. Wes Gething and Porter, the latter just weeks from becoming 17 and already the amateur middleweight boxing champion of Alberta, were on their way to prospect for gold and platinum and to buy fur on the Stranger River, a tributary of the Omineca.

It was spring, and the young sourdoughs went into the mountains by way of Summit Lake just outside Prince George where Bob's father, Herbert Porter, was a prominent fur buyer. Traveling in an 18-foot canoe with an outboard motor, they sleighed the craft across the still frozen lakes and embarked in it whenever they reached open water. At that time of the year as much water was flooding the Omineca as is ordinarily contained in the larger Nechako. In Black Canyon it was compressed into a roaring torrent, sometimes as cramped as 30 feet, rushing along with much greater velocity than the Nechako.

The two had proceeded approximately 700 feet up Black Canyon when they came to a rise of water. The canoe made it halfway up the lift until, even with the husky young Porter paddling in the bow, the current forced it backwards where the weight of the kicker caused it to upend in one of the roils.

Wes, seeing Porter swimming with one hand grasping the bow of the craft, grabbed a floating bedroll. Porter, appearing not in the least excited about his own situation, yelled to Wes to keep hold of the buoyant bedroll and to drift with the current. Doing this, Wes was soon out of sight of his apparently unconcerned companion. He was swept about 400 feet down the numbingly cold canyon until, drifting to within eight feet of shore, he made his way to land.

Exhausted and nearly freezing, he was unable to do anything more than keep a lookout for Porter as he stumbled along, shaking, to a McKinnon cabin they had noticed on their way in. Only the fact that the place was stocked with matches, shavings, and kindling, as is the custom in the North, saved him from death from exposure. There was also emergency food.

The formation of Black Canyon prevented Wes from seeing what had happened to Porter. The precipitous cliffs, his near-numb fatigue, and the deepening darkness prevented more than a cursory search until morning. Besides, inasmuch as Bob Porter had been within 20 feet of shore and had been swimming strongly with the canoe for support, Wes thought that Bob had made his own way to safety.

Looking for Porter at daybreak, Wes found no sign of him but did locate the canoe a short distance from the cabin; the motor had lodged on the bottom in about 10 feet of water. Finally deciding that going for help was the best thing to do, Wes made a rough log raft and succeeded in recovering the canoe, his only means of exit. In case of further accidents, before setting out he wrote a note describing the situation and leaned it against a candle holder on the cabin table. Still seeing no trace of his companion along the river, he determined to hurry to McKinnon's home cabin for assistance.

Half a dozen trappers immediately accompanied him back. Between the mouth of the Omineca and Black Canyon were hundreds of log jams, some consisting of just several large uprooted trees, but other jumbles being half a mile long and 30 feet high in places. Several days were put in searching the jams and dragging the river in what seemed to be likely spots. The paddle and a number of articles from the outfit were recovered, but the body wasn't located until some four months later when the receding water left it stranded well back on a gravel bar.

Jean and Wes put in a lot of time at the head of the Portage, where the generally serene flow of the Peace River was interrupted by Rocky Mountain Canyon. There was a cabin, more a cache, that the women used when there were a majority of men at hand. Neil Gething was the cook, and he was always bright and happy. He would rouse early in the morning, get the fire going, and call, "The sun is shining, the birds are singing, and, damn it, why don't you all get up?"

I had some personal experience with Neil's early-morning cooking when I was sleeping alone in the cookshack of King's old mine. He was manning the pots and pans. I'd usually still be drowsing when the preparations for early bacon, pancakes, and coffee got underway. So Neil, lonesome, would begin talking to himself. The "conversation" was so interesting that I soon found myself joining in.

Always most knowledgeable, Jean's father-in-law taught her many things: the constellations, how to find and identify fossils, and the names of plants and flowers. It was he who later first got me interested, too, in edible and medicinal wild plants and their uses. He was a friend to everyone, one of the truly greatest gentlemen I have ever had the good fortune to know.

Among the things I particularly remember from Mr. Gething's earlier teachings was how to make Hudson's Bay Tea, *ledum,* from the widely recognized evergreen of the same name. It is the leaves that are used, and these have a rustily thick woolliness clothing their inwardly rolling undersides. Used during the American Revolution, they provided a spicy and refreshing beverage. Once while I was helping Neil Gething get in a wagonful of firewood, I tried chewing a few of them and found the result both stimulating and thirst-quenching.

Mr. Gething built a riverboat which he called the *Queen*

Mary, and he even took the school nurse on a fishing trip for three days. He had a hard time living down that innocent incident. He kept horses and a wagon for hauling boats across the Portage whenever necessary.

"We made beautiful camps at the Portage," Jean recollects.

One of the most memorable trips Jean and Wes ever made on the upper Peace was after their motor gave out at Finlay Forks on a journey when they were carrying no passengers. They'd even left their only child with her grandparents in the Hope. Wes was hauling the mail then, so he borrowed another kicker at Finlay Forks to go up the Finlay River to Fort Graham and then back to the Forks.

There they returned it with thanks and then paddled all the way down to the Portage, 90 miles on waters that flowed gently, except for two rapids, through the Rockies from west to east.

"The current, of course, was strong enough to take the boat through," Jean told me. "We only used paddles to guide it. It was a tranquil trip. With no clamor of a motor, we could talk softly whenever we wished, and what wonderful, quiet, magnificent scenery! I hadn't realized how serene it could be without the racket of a motor and with the two of us alone to enjoy the beauty. Of all my memories, this one comes to my mind most often."

Jean and Wes had several experiences in getting moose out of season. They were canning such moose steaks one day at the Portage, with the big carcass out on the porch, when someone came along and said the game warden had landed at the Beattie cabin above them and would soon be over. So they frantically got the carcass into the woods and the canned meat into the cellar. The warden didn't notice anything. When the time came for dinner, Wes nonchalantly went down through the trapdoor and brought up a freshly canned portion of wild meat for the meal.

As mentioned previously, Beryl Prairie was named after the

tiny daughter of Jean and Wes Gething. Unlike the widely spread supposition, though, none of the Gething family had anything to do with this name. Joe MacNamee from Prince George had picture postcards made of a small lake he found on that open flat which runs from the Portage east of the north-south Butler Range. MacNamee is the one who dubbed it Beryl Lake after the Gethings' four-month-old baby.

It is also erroneous to suppose, as is widely done, that Wes and Jean Gething ever took up land on Beryl Prairie. They only ran a sawmill there in which, again contrary to public opinion, the other Gethings had no financial involvement.

Jean cooked for a dozen when the mill was functioning. Beryl was about five years old then, and that period was one of the only two full years before her retirement that Jean didn't teach school. Since 1904 when she'd started a kindergarten near Riding Mountain, Manitoba, close to where she was born, she had only those two hiatuses away from classrooms. That first school was at Nupawa, 25 miles from the town.

Jean's father, David McLarty, did take up land on Beryl Prairie, however, some three years after it was named.

Wes, the eldest Gething son, had a bad heart, for which reason he was honorably discharged from the Canadian Army during World War I. Because of his exuberance and his active life, few suspected that he had a problem.

He was on a trip to the original coal mine on the river with his father and Johnny Goodvin, apparently in the best of health. In fact, Wes had spent much of the previous day helping his younger brother, King, ready a snow sled. Still owning the only sawmill in the vicinity, he was already planning a large spring cut for the community. The three went to the mine for a sleigh load of the high-grade bituminous for Henry Stege, the H.B.C. post, and some of the local residents.

Not feeling too well after they reached the tunnel and buildings, Wes retired early. He awakened Goodvin during the early hours of the morning by mumbling in his sleep. Unable to arouse him, Goodvin called Neil who was bunking on the other side of the cabin. Wesley Gething, only 38 years old, died in his father's arms without regaining consciousness.

The sourdoughs for miles around attended the simple but impressive service at which the Reverend Noseworthy, Anglican pastor for the Peace River district, came from Fort St. John to officiate.

Jean, who has remained young and active, lived with Beryl part of the year in a log cabin across the street from the two-story frame house Wes had built from lumber sawed at his Beryl Prairie mill. Jean amicably sold the house to the family. When civilization reached Hudson Hope in recent years, Jean sold her cabin to B. C. Hydro which used it as an office.

Beryl eventually married the able Jim Linklater and started a family of her own in Dawson Creek. Jean has her own trailer at the present Linklater farm. Retired, Jean also maintains her own home in Dawson Creek, with a summer cabin built in 1962 at Moberly Lake.

"In his later years, Dudley Shaw left Hudson Hope only once that I know of," Jean told me. "This was when he came with the Kyllos to visit me at Moberly Lake. Dudley was so impressed with the cabin and its location that he couldn't understand my ever coming back to the city winters. He said, 'If I ever had such a noble spot, I'd never budge from it.' The cabin is right on the lake. I've spent many summers there."

The wide-reaching popularity Jean Victoria Gething achieved during a 35-year teaching career in Hudson Hope and elsewhere in the Peace River country—Taylor, Pouce Coupe, Prince George, Cache Creek, Kilkerran, Sunnybrook, Clayhurst, and finally at Dawson Creek where the Alaska Highway starts—was evidenced in 1959 when over 200 notables, friends, relatives, and former students attended a testimonial dinner held in her honor at the Dawson Creek elementary school.

"Speaking of my testimonial dinner," Jean recollects, "it surprised me that it got such wide newspaper coverage. *The Vancouver Province* had two writeups about it, one in the 'B. C. Roundup' and another on the women's page. *The Edmonton Journal* carried a story, with a picture of me receiving my inscribed silver tray. *The Calgary Herald* had an account of it though I never taught in Alberta, and there was even a half column in *The Montreal Gazette*. Yet all my 35 years of teaching, 31 years of which were in Hudson Hope and the Peace River area and the other four years in rural Prince George, was local."

A typical, practical, self-sufficient, down-to-earth schoolmarm like the best of them in Western fiction, Jean Gething has been traveling widely since her retirement from the Three-R years that included schoolhouses so primitive that one of them had nothing better than brown paper for windows.

| *17* |

Bear, Wolves, and Butterflies

▲

W‌HAT ABOUT peril from wild animals?

The fact is that in the Peace River country, as in most of domiciled North America, the most dangerous animals by far are domestic bulls. No one in Hudson Hope has ever been harmed by a bear, mountain lion, lynx, or any other wild animal, and certainly not by a wolf which with its high intelligence is the wariest of creatures.

The stress is on the word "wild." Black bear and grizzly in particular in the government parks, where they have lost much of their inbred fear of human beings, can be extremely dangerous indeed.

Joe Turner, whose ranch is a little more than a mile north of the town, was killed in his own corral by his bull. Leo Rutledge, long a leading outfitter for big game hunts, was marooned up a tree for several hours by a barnyard bull. Other local individuals have been threatened by bulls, who happen to be color blind and do not have to see red to become inflamed. Joe Barkley, Mel Kyllo, Matt Boe, the Gethings, Tompkins, Ardills, Murphys, and everyone who has been very much around bulls confirm that they are a lot more wary of them than of anything wandering wild in the bush.

The very rare wild grizzly can be dangerous. During a recent starving winter not far from the Hope an old grizzly came up behind the Indian who was tracking him in frigid weather, killed the man with a single blow to the skull, and ate part of the body. A friend of ours in the Game Department soon dispatched the man-eater. A younger brother of Gary Powell was chased over a cliff by an advancing grizzly which, once the youth was out of the way, did not pursue him. These are extremely infrequent cases, however.

Once, unarmed, I even talked a grizzly away from a moose we'd felled and left overnight. I have inadvertently found myself between a black bear and her tan twin cubs. But by remaining calm, staying still, and talking quietly I persuaded her to circle closely around me as was made necessary by the terrain, join her youngsters which were as scrawny as monkeys, and go away.

The only time I have ever really been in trouble with a wild animal was when I accidentally cornered a browsing bull moose up a narrow blind canyon while hunting and finally had to add him to our larder with a shot at close quarters. But nothing like this has happened any other time, to me or to any local sourdough I know, and I never hesitate to take a nap wherever I may be in the wilds.

Polar bear, unprovoked, will sometime stalk and kill humans, but they are far north among the ice floes of the Arctic.

It was dunned into me early during my wilderness living that the worst thing an individual can do when confronted by a wild animal is to panic and run. To give an everyday example, some dogs will chase moving vehicles. But put on the brakes, traffic permitting, and they will quickly lose interest.

There was a grizzly in Rocky Mountain Canyon all of one winter. Fred Monteith was one of those who spotted him. Grizzlies sleep less than black bears during the snowy months. That winter Wesley and Jean Gething were camped in an early coal mine cabin, known by the family as The Igloo. Wes was trapping that year, and it was one of the very few winters that Jean wasn't teaching school.

King Gething stayed overnight with them on one occasion and started for the family's Portage cabin after lunch. He was back within an hour. The dry snow of the North was particularly loose at that time. (Vena always has to use water when she makes snowmen.) King followed a peculiar track which seemed as if an injured man had been crawling. Something caused him to glance up, and he saw a massive grizzly standing on his hind legs, looking at him.

Acting very cautiously so as not to alarm the beast, King warily eased the heavy pack off his shoulders and began walking backwards. The grizzly didn't move, so King finally turned and, without wasting any time, returned to The Igloo where Wes and he got rifles and started back. But it was becoming dark by then and snowing, so, retrieving the pack, they came back to Jean. The brothers hunted all the next day, but the flakes had filled in all the tracks.

Black bears are both the comedians and the pests of our wilderness. Lured by odors such as the lingering aroma of bacon, they are often destructive once one has left a camp.

Wes and King once landed at a mining cabin to find that in their absence bears had broken the windows, entered, and in their search for food wrecked everything from stovepipe and dishes to bunks. Hungry themselves, the two did what they could to get a stove fire going safely, put on some meat and potatoes to simmer, slung on their rifles, and went after the intruders. They didn't find any. But when they got back they found the cabin vandalized again. A black bear had upset things, knocked down the stovepipe once more, and even eaten the meal they left cooking.

Some years while fall harvesting was going on at Beryl Prairie and elsewhere north of the Hope, black bears were a real nuisance. They would roll in the grain, knock over stooks, and carry away sheaves. The settlers felt they had to defend their livelihoods, and as a consequence bear meat graced many cabin tables that autumn and winter.

Wes and Jean Gething were once camping at their water-wheel sawmill up the Canyon at Johnson Creek—a mill which some years later I helped Larry Gething and his dad dismantle and take back to the Hope by sleigh over the river ice. Jean had brought along a small Dresden china teapot, as at that time she disliked the common backwoods practice of brewing the beverage in large tin cans.

A wedding gift, the teapot was white and painted with flowers in a tasteful variety of colors. When Wes and Jean left for town, they planned to come right back. Their routine changed, however, and Jean asked her father-in-law to bring the teapot to her on his next trek upriver.

By the time Neil Gething got back to the Johnson Creek cabin, bears had broken through the windows and made a mess of things, smashing many of the dishes and even the mirror. The teapot had disappeared. Neil tracked the intruders into the woods and, astonished, was overjoyed to find the lovely Dresden piece unharmed. The way he figured it, a bruin had been sufficiently attracted by the bright beauty of the little teapot to carry it carefully in its mouth over the windowsill and into the forest before tiring of it.

The black bears around the Hope come in two similar varieties. Some of them are brown, a hue that makes anyone who encounters one of them look cautiously for the telltale grizzly shoulder hump. Jean was driving back from Moberly Lake one recent fall when she came upon a black and a brown bear fighting. The blackie, although only about half the size of his adversary, was a real scrapper. The combat remained pretty even until, after about 20 minutes, the animals noticed the car and disappeared.

Then there are the moose. One night King Gething left a group on a sandy beach during a river trip. One of the party, a cheechako by the name of Cecil, decided he was going to stand sentry with a gun by the campfire all night to keep animals away from Jean, her sister, and the young Beryl. During the middle of the night Jean was awakened by something just outside their tent.

Looking through the netting, she saw two long pale legs, so at first she thought it was some man trying to gain entry. Then she realized it was the back end of a moose who was standing there. She quietly got up and drove the cow moose and its calf away for fear the sleeping Cecil might awaken and shoot them. Of course, he didn't believe her in the morning.

"Aw-wa-oooo-ooh." The close-at-hand howls of timber wolves, pleasantly spine-tingling to us in the moonlight, have a wild and rousing sound to them in the silent spaces. "Aw-wa-oooooo."

Vena and I have always been thrilled by the long deep howls ever since we heard them our first night alone in our first log cabin. City folk, frightened by utterly fictitious timber wolves attacking humans, have greatly maligned these magnificent creatures. Wolves are often big, alarmingly so to those who do not understand them, in our area weighing up to 180 pounds. But they are so cautious that we seldom get a look at them.

Yet we have been very close to them on a number of occasions. The first time was when we were tracking a moose in the snow amid the foothills above our cabin on one of our first British Columbia hunts. I knew the moose was nearby because there were fresh signs of his nipping the tender tips of poplar saplings. Then the hoofprints began to zigzag, a sign that he was about to lie down.

Staying downwind, we left the trail and circled so that hopefully he would not get our scent. When we met up with the big tracks again, I found two wolves following them. At the sight of us, they angled away into the brush in a series of short, sharp turns with all the alacrity of all-American broken-field runners. It was perhaps 10 minutes later, to conclude the story, that the moose stood up in a small dense stand of spruce where he had been snoozing. There was a bough in my line of vision, so Vena took the shot that assured our meat supply.

Another occasion was a late-arriving winter whose approach had been warmed by so many chinooks that Vena had to can what game we had in the cache. We were ravenous for fresh meat. So when a wolf pack awoke us at night, howling directly across the river, I knew they must have just made a fresh kill, probably a moose.

We weren't likely to get one closer, so I hurriedly left the warmth of my sleeping bag and started to get dressed. Vena, not about to let me go alone, quickly followed. The timber wolves eased into the blackness at our approach, leaving a nearly intact, dry, fat cow moose. We built a fire and, butchering the animal and taking the liver, we decided to wait until daylight to dismember and pack the meat across to our cache. Although the wolves must have been hungry, too, there were no further signs of the pack. We knew they'd be able to roam far and wide to find other food in areas we'd never hunt.

"Just a couple of years ago," Jean Gething told me the other day, "I was driving out to the farm with Beryl and her husband Jim Linklater, when our headlights caught the glowing eyes of a huge cow moose and her newly born calf. The calf was sprawled in the middle of the road and didn't seem able to get up. Jim started to see if it were hurt. The mother came charging the pickup. With his door still open, Jim reversed the truck in a hurry."

They had never before encountered such a large cow moose, and she charged several times, always stopping short of the headlights. They patiently waited for what seemed to be close to an hour for the calf to rise and wobble to the side of the road.

Then they safely passed it. The cow moose, however, ran in front of the pickup for nearly two miles before she swerved into the bush.

Big, hard-working, extremely religious Matt Boe—who in his youth held down a job along with Joe Barkley and Dennis Murphy at Wes Gething's sawmill—married Erna Turner after her first husband was killed by his bull in 1936. Shortly after the wedding black bears started carrying off their pigs in the night. You can't jack bears with a strong light as you can moose and deer who stand motionless, their eyes fascinated by the beam. Bears just tumble away from the illumination. Nothing halted the ravages on the Boe pigsty until Matt reluctantly got permission from the Game Department to use poison. After that there was no more trouble.

Muskrats, pack rats, varying hare that change color with the season, and butterflies? Jean once taught school 25 miles from the nearest town, and the only meat she had was the hare she shot from her doorway and the dark-meated muskrats she shot on the river. A neighbor with a trapper's license sold the pelts for her. The so-called rabbits come in cycles, and there were years they were so thick that they once chewed Chinook's lariat tether into three pieces one night at the Portage. They've been known locally to fell a tent over a sleeping sourdough by gnawing the perspiration-salted guy ropes.

As for pack rats who drop what they are carrying to bear away something else, perhaps a brightly shining key, they are noisome, ill-smelling pests to boot. Transfixing the animals with a flashlight, sourdoughs shoot them with a .22 or catch them by placing a trap under a board slanted against the wall.

Fortunately we were visited by few porcupines. Those that came by were an even greater nuisance, especially as Bushman hated them and killed them, in the process getting his muzzle and head full of barbed quills that had to be removed with pliers. The dog was so large and powerful that it was difficult to hold him still during the necessary proceedings. Once when I was alone I got him lying down with his back against a birch and tied him backwards that way.

A porky climbed the screen door of a Gething cabin one day, and Jean couldn't get out with her baby until someone switched it away. They are so avid for salt that they are forever gnawing canoe paddles, toilet seats, and the like. One nibbled Jean's umbrella when she was lying out in the sun one midday.

Even wild horses can cause trouble. Once Art Holman, on his railroad surveying trip to the Hope, lifted his tent flap and was startled to find himself eyeball to eyeball, except for a big nose, with a wild stallion.

"He made a dash for the woods and knocked down the tent," Art told me. "What a mess on our blankets! He had been there for hours, seeking refuge from the vicious flies that also plagued the moose. The next day we found he had been in again, chewing up our blankets, towels, and clothes, so we decided we would have to do something about it. One of the party was a wrangler. He roped the stallion and, with our amateur help, gelded him. We didn't see him or his harem again."

Legendary North American snowmen and savage apelike creatures? The sourdoughs delight in tall tales, and many of their listeners have even more vivid imaginations. Different concrete things, other than attention-seeking, also give rise to such accounts. A trapper friend of ours, for instance, once used real ingenuity to frighten away some Indians who were disputing the ownership of his line. He hammered together weird wooden contraptions with which he made lifelike and successfully scary tracks in the mud and slush. Others have let gullible greenhorns see them in terrifying Hallowe'en-like garb. It has been long proved to reasonable people that such yarns have no foundation in fact.

Butterflies? Hundreds of frail, black-and-orange monarchs wing their way above the Hudson Hope area in spring and fall, migrating from and to a 9,500-foot Mexican volcano where they winter. On the 3,000-mile trip, the colorful butterflies fly at an altitude of just 15 feet, only stopping by day to feed on flowers and at night clustering in trees along the route.

Lepidopterists believe that the monarch butterfly evolved in Mexico thousands of years ago. As the glaciers melted, they apparently expanded their breeding grounds further and further north, and through the alchemy of life created generations endowed with the secret of their species: how to return to their ancient home.

| *18* |

North of Night

▲

Summers arrived with their seemingly never-ending daylight, with twilights ebbing into dawns. The rain was as scant as snow had been, this being essentially a semiarid country. Yet enough moisture fell to make patches of thick brush except under the taller trees. There, green screens kept the sunlight off the earth on which pine needles muffled the pounding of our horses' hooves.

Vegetables grew startlingly large while there was no real night, shadows merely lengthening in the quietude until the sun shone again. This was good, for in addition to the free-for-the-eating munificence of edible wild plants, we wanted some domestic vegetables to store in our root cellar, underneath a trapdoor in the floor of our log home. Our current-free wilderness refrigerator was below the frost level.

So we spaded the small area of sun-warmed land we required for our beans, potatoes, lettuce, radishes, cabbages, and peas. We'd soon discovered that if we'd live simply and eat little except the crop we raised, and raise no more than we ate, we would need to cultivate only a small plot of ground. We could do all the necessary "farm work," as it were, at odd hours in the summer.

"It is not necessary," we agreed with Thoreau, "that a man should earn his living by the sweat of his brow unless he sweats easier than I do."

One of our neighbors in Hudson Hope, felling some of the

burned and seasoned poplar and lodgepole pine between us and town, shot a young bull moose on which the fat was already well formed. He insisted that both Dudley and we accept quarters. His wife and children were visiting relatives in Ontario, and he didn't want to bother with more meat than he could eat before it spoiled.

We could not devour enough of our share that fast either, so we went to Neil Gething for advice. Riding the back way up Bull Creek to the ridge that led past Larry Gething's trapping cabin on King's mining road, we followed that to the mine where we found King and Bill Currie overhauling an old truck engine for use that fall on the mine trestle. They were busy near the elaborate machine shop, where a gasoline-fueled generator was charging the thin, flat, nickeled batteries for the miners' safety lights, and where there was a shower. A powder hut sat on a knoll a safe distance away.

"How have the bears been?" I asked King.

"There's been the odd one," King said, "but there never has been a concentration of them since you thinned them down. That was a lifesaver, by Jove."

"We want to get your father's recipe for canning moose meat," Vena told him. "Vesta and some of the others around town say it's the best they've ever eaten."

"Dad's boiling the kettle in the cookshack," King said, pushing his inevitable brown hat further back on his wide brow. Colin Campbell, trucker with a large family and a black-haired wife named Anne, told us he'd come upon Quentin Franklin Gething one time seated in a huge basin of hot water, happily singing and sponging himself, with his felt hat still on. "It's time to knock off for a spot, Bill, don't you figure?"

"There's always time for tea when you're around," said the bespectacled, comparatively slight Currie.

"You'll stay overnight, of course," King was saying. "There's a couple of extra sleeping bags in the guest cabin. Then we can have a few hands of bridge. You're good at it, I understand, Vena."

"She's a lot better bridge player than I am," I told them, watching Vena walk past the screen door that King hospitably held open. She moved as gracefully as if she were dancing. "All I know is what I learned during a summer of free-lance writing in Greenwich Village. That was until I got a wire from Ben Shlyen, offering me the job of New England editor of *Boxoffice* if I'd return to Boston in time to get out the next weekly edition."

"You went?" King asked.

"I went," I said. "That's where I first saw Vena, dancing in the Elida Ballet."

Neil Gething, who was already distributing a handful of enameled cups on the long table, greeted us and added a couple more to the array.

Although we had never thought of him as that, I realized that he was an old man. Yet his vibrant voice, clear eyes, healthy red cheeks, and neatly combed white hair above a white mustache seemed infused with impregnable vigor.

"You're going to be with us overnight, Vena and Brad, I hope," he echoed. I recognized the beefy smell from the stove. "Bill got a young bear who'd been plaguing us, and I've a big roast in the oven."

I looked at Vena, and she nodded.

"That'll be great, thanks," I agreed. "I'll picket the horses in that tall grass. They'll do fine. We already watered them on the way in."

"We want to find out how you can moose," Vena said.

"Nothing to it," Neil Gething said obligingly. "Glad to share what little I've learned with you, Vena, although you probably know most of it already."

"That's very nice of you to say so," Vena responded.

We were already seating ourselves on the benches at either side of the long table.

Once when I was the dummy during the bridge game that evening, I got up and stood in the coolness of the doorway. Clouds were scudding like spots of watercolor across the last ruby glow of the long since sunken sun.

I don't know how long I lingered there, but when I realized that the bridge game was giving way to another round of tea, rain suddenly exploded, pounding like Alaska Highway gravel on the windows. Vena put an arm around me.

The sudden storm blurred the gleam of the lifting moon until, in the downpour, my mind played games. The lifeless spikes of burned trees on the Bullhead mountainside that slanted above us were like stick voyageurs. Then an even more violent downpour erased them like figures on a college blackboard.

As we watched, the storm that had appeared like a wet phantom was swallowed by the maw of night as abruptly as it had come. Toward the east, the lights of Fort St. John seemed to rush in our direction like a phantasmagoria. Nearer were the gaps in the nearby ridge across the river from where our cabin waited.

The odd drops of moisture from the trees splashed like footsteps in a quiet manor. The orange moon, still low enough to be magnified by the earth's atmosphere, stole among the clouds like a distant searchlight. What remained of the breezes about the outbuildings quieted, and the brilliant night became as still as if smothered beneath a wet gloved palm.

The woods were already dry again when we rode back down through them the next morning, although here and there Chinook's and Cloud's hooves spattered through placid pools of water.

Back at our log home, I cut the remaining parts of the moose into inch-square cubes, while Vena scalded her jars in a washtub of boiling water. Then she melted a generous amount of bacon grease in our largest Dutch oven and added the pieces of meat, along with salt and a little water. She covered the heavy cast iron receptacle with its weighty lid, and we put it into the oven of our wood-burning range. She set an oven thermometer beside it.

"There," she said, backhanding a wave of brown hair gracefully from in front of her hazel eyes. "Now to cook the meat at about 200° for approximately five hours."

As Neil had suggested, she looked at the contents from time to time, occasionally adding a little water from the steaming teakettle when the meat seemed to be getting too dry. The aroma filling the cabin became more and more intriguing, and I gave the salivating Bushman a liberally meated bone to gnaw.

After five hours Vena, with my help, put the Dutch oven on top of the stove. The chunks of meat proved to be tender by that time. She removed them and made gravy with the liquor that remained in the bottom of the utensil, adding flour and stirring until the fat absorbed it. Then she put in boiling water until the gravy seemed to be of the right consistency.

While the moose had been cooking, Vena had caramelized some sugar in a frying pan. She added seething water to it and poured it into the mixture along with a little cider vinegar and some dry mustard. The result was a rich brown gravy. At this point she tipped the meat into the gravy, banged on the iron lid, and got everything simmering on top of the stove.

"That tastes perfect," I said afterwards.

"Mr. Gething made it sound so simple," she replied. "I couldn't go wrong. It's all thanks to him. What a wonderful gentleman!"

We found we liked the Hudson Hope summers least of all the seasons. Our favorite time was spring. Then came autumn, followed by winter.

Surprisingly perhaps, the summers in the Far North are sometimes uncomfortably hot. Because of the length of the day there is little relief at night. We did have the benevolence of the river, which moderated the temperature and which encouraged breezes that kept away most of the mosquitoes.

The remainder of the winged biters we repelled with Deet, developed by the U. S. Department of Defense and given me, as it was to others, to test. Incidentally, we found the most effective mixture was half and half with alcohol. The insects in the Hudson Hope area aren't ordinarily all that bad, however, and there are none of the little black flies that make many parts of the thickly forested Northeast difficult to endure.

Summertime brought the pilgrims, the cheechako visitors who sometimes became as pesky as the no-see-ums which appeared at dusk and at dawn. This was when we were particularly engrossed in our own activities, including my writing and Vena's illustrating some of my books. She also sold oil paintings and watercolors on the side. The visitors were always interesting once we got into conversation with them, but they often did interrupt our busy schedules.

I thought wryly about all our acquaintances back in Boston who had wondered what we would ever find to do with our spare time in the wilderness, away from the theaters, night clubs, and other social institutions.

When the wild berries ripened, Vena and I joined in picking basket upon basket of blackberries, saskatoons, blueberries, currants, raspberries, and all the rest, not to forget the early succulent strawberries. Savoring those red fruits, I kept remembering Dr. William Butler's saying, "Doubtless God could have made a better berry, but doubtless God never did." Another naturalist had added, "I had rather have one pint of wild strawberries than a gallon of tame ones." So would we.

Then there were other tidbits such as the ripe sweet fruit of False Solomon's Seal—whatever was left, that is, that the horses hadn't nipped away. These taste like soda pop.

Occasionally, especially among the thick bushes on the flat above our cabin, a surprised black bear would suddenly rear up in front of us, then as quickly crash out of our hearing.

Sometimes, crossing the river in the *Peacemaker,* we'd lie on our stomachs and watch the beaver work on their dams and houses. Usually by the time we were beginning to feel rich with leisure, some vagrant breeze would take them our scent. An oldster would smack the water in warning with his flat broad tail, and they'd all disappear, like small boys of yesteryear, scurrying naked from their swimming pool at the sound of a stranger, perhaps a girl.

Many of the berries we gathered we ate on the spot or enjoyed with our meals. Others Vena turned into jam, marmalade, and syrup for our hot sourdough pancakes. There were also jar after colorful jar of canned berries for enjoying during the snowy days of winter. That fruit, which too much cold would have frozen and burst, we stowed in our root cellar.

It all gave us more satisfaction than we'd ever dreamed of in our more optimistic moments in Boston. Perhaps, I thought, it's especially in the wild places, where one has to be self-sufficient, that the simpler things of life are really esteemed.

| *19* |

No Ladies of the Evening

▲

THERE WERE no ladies of the evening as such in the Hudson Hope area. The world's oldest profession was practiced instead as a part of homemaking. The bachelors of the bush, the lonely trappers and prospectors, were often glad for the opportunity of savoring cooking other than their own and of enjoying some of the comfort and relaxation of a warm home life. So a few of the bigger-hearted single women of the community lived with them and were their housekeepers.

It was a completely normal and respected practice of the country, and it did much to improve the tone of living. After all, it got to be a mighty lonesome proposition for many a healthy, robust sourdough to dwell by himself in the stimulating splendor of the colored aurora borealis and the cannonading of the river ice and the green trees, as they cracked in the intense cold which was sometimes more than 60° below zero Fahrenheit. Then there was the even more rousing sweep of the great flocks of swans, Canada geese, and sandhill cranes as they babbled northward in the glory of the early spring.

Here in the North, men will meet in the course of a lonely winter where their trap lines intersect; they've often not been close to another human for months. Delighted to see each other, most of them will chatter for about an hour and a half. The rest of the night they will camp together, neither of them saying a word. And in the morning they'll part in silent understanding for another stretch of solitude.

In self-defense, nearly every male sourdough gets to be a better than passable cook; so too are even the happily married wilderness men who are periodically alone among the far-flung circles of cabins on their trap lines, or traveling and camping by themselves while seeking the mother lode. It was a spectacle never to be forgotten by some of the visiting sportsmen from Outside to happen upon a group of rugged bushmen, sitting around a communal stove and swapping recipes. Incidentally, it is still the practice of many a lone trapper and prospector to take to bed with him the covered receptacle holding his rising sourdough makings. That's how he keeps the dough warm enough to remain active.

Even the venerable Hudson's Bay Company sought to increase the confidence of its bachelor post managers with the unequivocal statement that "The best cooks in the world are men," although it did somewhat temper the assertion a few paragraphs along in their standard manual with the advice not to use the dishcloth to wipe the stove.

Some of the early sourdoughs, such as Dudley Shaw, made their way north by cooking for parties of one kind or another. But the most renowned cook of the settlement was Ted Boynton who had handled the pots and pans for the hunting parties of Jim Ross, then the foremost big game outfitter of the region, and for the Charles Bedeau expedition. His restaurant, next to the Fergusons' precisely built hotel, was enlivened by such signs as: "Don't make fun of our coffee. You'll be old and weak yourself someday," and the chuckle-arousing, "Use less sugar and stir like hell. We don't mind the noise."

It was the depression years, and the understanding game wardens didn't mind the inhabitants keeping themselves in meat so long as nobody wasted any. In cold weather Ted always had moose quarters hanging in his cache, and when we shot our first moose, it was Ted who drove up in his sleigh with Dudley and Marion and Dave Cuthill as passengers, unhitched his team, and with one cayuse, the one from the unsuccessful Bedeau trek, skidded the animal down to our cabin one Sunday morning for the total sum of five dollars.

Ted, who was already well supplied, declined with thanks our offer to share our prize. So except for one forequarter to Dudley and some back steaks to Dave and Marion, we had the entire animal with which to finish out the winter, with some left over to can for the warm months.

It was Ted, as much as anyone, who impressed on us that game was so precious and so hard to come by that it was wrong to squander any part of it. Even today when I see anyone disregarding some of the less popular ducks, alleging that the fowl taste is too fishy or gamy, I remember how Ted used to turn birds of this sort into prize fare.

I guess one group from San Antonio thought they had Ted backed into a corner when they brought in a couple of mud hens. One of the Texas hunters admitted that he had tried to eat mud hen before. He allowed that if the part he wound up with had gone over the fence last, someone must have given it a boost.

Perhaps it was the aroma mingling with the pine-scented air from the direction of Ted's cookstove, a handy portable affair still manufactured by the Sims interests in Lovell, Wyoming. Perhaps it was mainly inquisitiveness, for a mud hen, although friendly with its family and all, is ordinarily about as tender and tasty as a worn-out innersole. In any event, there was no need that dusk for a second, "Come and git it or I'll throw it away."

On a couple of stainless steel plates reposed the waterfowl, tanned and redolent, appearing as tempting as mallard and smelling no less inviting than plump ptarmigan. One disbeliever injected his fork doubtfully into a breast. Steaming, savory meat fell temptingly away from the bone. Everyone turned to ardently.

"Even a loon don't cook up too bad," Ted told Vena and me,

and later proved the fact, "if a yahoo don't try to gentle it aitch-for-leather. So don't throw mud hens or any such critters away, 'specially in times like these. Cram 'em with onions. B'il real easy for three hours. Then start brand new with a crumb stuffing. Tuck a lot of sow belly where it'll do the most good, and roast nice and quietlike until a hungry man can't wait no longer."

Big game kidneys, usually discarded, are real tidbits, as King Gething assured us once when we were up by Finlay Forks, on the Peace River across from Mount Selwyn, camped on the property of our friend, Count Ignatief, who had escaped to Canada during the Russian revolution. "I like them simmered awhile with butter, cloves, salt, celery if we have any, and a mite of onion. Matter of fact, let's get them in the frypan before someone else shows up."

Divide or cut the kidneys into pieces about the size of chicken hearts. All you have to do with bear kidneys to accomplish this is to pull away the connecting membrane. Let the meat and other ingredients broil over low heat until tender. The handiest way to settle proportions is by taste. These kidneys are particularly flavorful, with their gravy, on steaming mounds of mashed potato or with hot crusty bannocks, streaming with butter or margarine.

Cooking game can teach self-sufficiency. Then if the day ever comes when you are dependent upon your own resources for survival, you should be able to get along handsomely. But one has to go about such cookery capably, for wild meat, with certain exceptions, lacks fat; that'll have to be supplied by your own efforts.

Too, the active existence of game animals living in the unconfined further places can make their resulting steaks and roasts dry and stringy if certain provisions are not made to overcome these deficiencies. Yet it is all most worthwhile. Prepared the right way, wild meat brings a woodland freedom and savor to even the deepest concrete canyon.

"Many campers would pass by a porcupine, on which there is even a bounty in some places. Still he is the purest of all vegetarians," the late dean of the outdoor writers, Colonel Townsend Whelen, told me when we were writing a book together. "My memory goes back to when Bone Andrews, one of the last of the old mountain men of the breed of Jim Bridger, and I were compelled to spend a couple of weeks not far from where Prince George is now, where there was no game.

"At the end of that time we had the worst case of meat fever you can imagine. So we saddled up our little pack train and made tracks for higher altitudes and game country. On the way up I shot a porcupine. I skinned it, starting at the smooth belly, and tied it to my saddle.

"That night we made it into a stew. First, we cut it into pieces and boiled these for an hour. Then we added a handful of rice, some salt, a dozen small dumplings of biscuit dough, and put the lid on that to boil 20 minutes longer. This was tall country. With the air pressure lessening with the altitude, the higher you climb, the longer you have to boil. We finally finished by adding a little flour to thicken the gravy and by stirring in a teaspoon of curry powder.

"Then the two of us sat down and finished the whole pot at one sitting. That pot held nine quarts and was full."

20

King of the Halfway

▲

"MY SETTLING on the Halfway River, just east of the Hope, was the result of a primal instinct that was associated with a long history of agrarian ancestors. It was also the yearning of a youngster who could not afford even to feed a stray dog, to have a chunk of land that was his own," Philip F. Tompkins told me.

Phil, known as "King of the Halfway" by some of the local citizenry, was born of parents who homesteaded in southern Saskatchewan in the early 1880s. He came west in 1908 to Calgary, the great stampede town of Alberta, then north to the Peace River and the Halfway in 1919 after serving three years in World War I. The important Halfway River, a great stream when in flood, was so named because it is approximately midway between Hudson Hope and Fort St. John.

Phil settled on the eastern side, a particularly strategic point before the building of a bridge during the winter of 1935. Because the stream became nigh impassable when the ice was forming in the autumn and when it was breaking up in the spring, Phil and Emily Tompkins opened their doors to the many travelers who then were stranded there.

An example of the Tompkinses' hospitality is attested by Jean Gething. Charlie Townsend, an Englishman, was driving a sleigh with Lloyd and Lillian Gething, still weak from the flu, and Jean and her four-month-old daughter Beryl as passengers. They were traveling from the Hope to Cache Creek, where Jean was teaching school, when the sleigh broke down just west of the Halfway River. The night temperature was a snapping 35° below zero, and the snow was up to everyone's ankles when they had to get out and walk.

Having stopped at the Ardills' on the way in and given them the bug, the Gethings did not want to bother them again. Afraid of the epidemic, others refused them haven. So they continued on to the Tompkinses', Jean in the lead with the heavy child in her arms and Lloyd and Lillian faltering behind.

Phil answered the rapping. Jean breathlessly explained the situation, asking if they could stay in the barn for that night until the sleigh could be repaired.

"We've never turned anyone from our door, and we're not going to start now," Phil said. "Come on into the house. If we get the flu, we get the flu, but come into the house. We'll just put another can of creosote on the stove."

Phil and Emily treated them royally. Then the next day, after temporary sleigh repairs, the vehicle broke down again at the top of the tough, long Tompkins hill. It was Jean who made four trips down the steep incline after blankets and other necessities, finally resorting to the Tompkinses again where she waited for the mail carrier. That fellow finally arrived, drove Jean up the hill this time, and eventually took the four of them to Cache Creek, Townsend staying with the disabled sleigh and his team.

"That," Jean told us, "was just one of the numerous examples of Phil and Emily Tompkins' more than usual northern hospitality. We can never thank them enough."

"The summer of 1919, while I was still employed on the staff at Jasper Park," Phil told me when reminiscing about his early years, "I met my brother who had just returned after fighting the Bolsheviki in Siberia. This meeting was in Edmonton upon his discharge.

"Learning that he and several of his army friends were contemplating going to the Peace, I joined them, first going back to

Jasper where I got a never-terminated six-month leave of absence."

Phil and Emily Tompkins were married in Bristol, England on May 29, 1915, following Phil's discharge from a hospital after wounds received at the battle of St. Jean (Ypres) on April 22nd. His bride was Emily Amelia Budd, a member of a very old Celtic family. One of her relatives, a Dr. Budd, was the prototype of Dr. Watson of the Sherlock Holmes stories. He had been a college mate of author A. Conan Doyle.

"Anyway, I got my family and at once proceeded to get together a carload of necessities. My brother joined me later at Peace River and helped load our belongings on the *D. A. Thomas.* So we started upriver on that stern-wheeler. I stayed below deck with the stock and other possessions, but my brother put in his time talking with the passengers, most of whom were experienced Peace Riverites.

"He advised me that on the third day we should unload at the Halfway River boat landing. This was done, and the *D. A. Thomas* continued upriver. While we were getting our camp organized, we had a visit from a young fellow who introduced himself as Hazzard Cadenhead. He told us that his mother with three children had been here since 1911. Their farmstead was adjacent to the boat landing where we were encamped, and we were invited to dine with them all that evening.

"When I entered the house and met the mother, I got a jolt. Somewhere I had met her before. She was no ordinary-looking woman. The connection came to me while we were having supper, a really sumptuous repast. It had been a somewhat unfortunate encounter.

"The fall of 1911 I moved to Edmonton from Calgary where I had spent my first years in the West. As an assistant bookkeeper in an electrical construction firm, I had been given the job of cleaning up some delinquent accounts. One of the little two-bit bills just around the corner from our concern got my early attention. There I ran into Mrs. Cadenhead who owned and operated a two-story brick duplex in the very heart of the city, as well as a half section (320 acres) five miles west of Edmonton.

"She didn't pay the 25 cents. A roomer had burned out a fuse and called us in. Actually, her son could have replaced the faulty fuse. Oh, yes, she remembered the encounter, and I had to admit that I was the punk collector."

It developed that the center of the flat was owned by two Scots, Forfar and McDonald. Ed Forfar was a grandson of the proprietor of Pears Soap. He later represented the British Columbia Police in Hudson Hope, before the Mounties took over in later years. McDonald was an elderly sheepherder who was declining rapidly and who died during the coming winter.

"My brother and I finally bought them out later that fall," Phil resumed. "I stayed to operate their establishment, while my brother returned to Edmonton to teach school in order to accumulate the cash for our deal with the Scots. The rigors of that 1919-1920 winter bankrupted us as well as many another of the early settlers, the Cadenheads amongst the rest. In the years of the Depression, Mrs. Cadenhead lost her Edmonton holdings, valued at a quarter of a million dollars in 1911, because of the $40,000 dollars she had borrowed to finance their odyssey to the Peace, only to find the Scots squatting in the middle of their projected holdings.

"The Cadenhead land, a half section and a fraction, finally wound up in the possession of a grandson from whom we bought it. In addition, I subsequently filed on land, originally leased by the Cadenheads, as a homestead and Soldier's Grant. This completed the entire area on the Halfway flat, a total of some 1,500 acres. The land in the valley west of the Halfway was acquired through the Second World War army credits of our sons. Our present holdings are now in the neighborhood of 12,000 acres."

Phil summed it all up for me during the writing of this book when he said, "I've known some of the famous and have been aware and knowledgeable of all the personalities who have crossed the Canadian stage of life during the years, pretty well understanding what I have witnessed."

Phil Tompkins, King of the Halfway, had built his castles in the air. Now he has put the foundations under them.

| *21* |

The Indians

▲

THE CREE AND BEAVER INDIANS in the 1920s often camped on the outskirts of Hudson Hope in their smoke-hued teepees, made not of skins as in the old days but of the white man's canvas. The patient squaws, the workers, still cooked over campfires as usual, however. Many of them chewed tobacco or snoose. They spat the juice unconcernedly wherever they might be, perhaps beside a suspended mulligan pot of game meat and vegetables which they were stirring.

They still baked their fowl unopened in clay in the hot ashes of their campfires, inasmuch as the heat turns the entrails into neat, little, easily discarded wads. Generally they dined on meat and on bannock—the white man's frypan bread composed of flour, lard, salt, baking powder, and then water. The trading posts sold lots of flour and baking powder to the Indians.

They also retailed numerous muzzle-loaders to the Indians, particularly to the older braves. The reason was that the government freely supplied the tribes with black powder, shot for birds and small game, ball for moose and bear and sheep, wadding, and other necessities.

In the springtime the ribbon departments would do a large business with the Indians in Hudson Hope, especially as the younger redmen liked to festoon their saddles and bridles with bright streamers. Ordinarily by the time the tribes shifted to the berry-thick areas, the Hudson's Bay post and Henry Stege were ribbonless.

It was still the era of treaty payments. The Union Jack was usually fluttering in the prevailing west wind. The Indian agent generally sat at a table with long sheets of the names of the eligibles and an alluring stack of brand new one-dollar bills. A provincial policeman, such as our friend Ray Sandy who later became a Fort St. John judge, stood at attention. In a partial circle, at a respectful distance, were the Crees and the Beavers.

Indians were legally prohibited from purchasing alcohol, but imagination was a great thing. One year young Lloyd Gething set up a stand to sell nonalcoholic root beer at a few cents a glass. In no time at all Indians were weaving all over town, crowding with fresh enthusiasm about the never-neglected ribbon counters, the stacks of cotton dresses, the penny candies, and the canned sausage-like meats. A number of the braves later utilized strings of empty cans to clatter behind their horses and attract the curious moose and deer.

Some church dignitary was always present to get his donation of a dollar apiece, which was perhaps just as well for otherwise the money went for frivolities or gambling. Campfires burned late in front of the teepees. Dancing, ki-yi-yiing Indians mixed their singing and yipping with the cacophony of drums.

In latter days a few Indians were generally outside at the Hudson Hope dances, peeking in at the revelers and taking advantage of those of the sourdoughs who, generous in their exuberance, shared the bottles from which they'd gone outside for a nip.

Most of the Hudson Hope Indians lived either near Harry Garbitt at Moberly Lake, two days south on the other side of the river, or by Teddy Green on the upper Halfway River system, a good two days north of the village. Harry was a Scot, Ted an Englishman. Both of them were our friends.

The truck which had originally brought us to Hudson Hope had been heavied with Indian freight, later taken in a sleigh hauled by two large work horses, Blaze and Queen, and driven by Joe Barkley to its destination at Ted's. We've accompanied Joe to Teddy's over the winter trail, slashed through frozen muskeg and often thick brush, stopping overnight at Graveyard Creek. This is a clear mountain stream whose minerals combine to make the best coffee I've ever tasted in any part of the world.

Graveyard Creek, where there has long been a cabin and stable, got its name when B. C. Brady accidentally ran over one of his children with a sleigh. He buried the child there on a knoll by an open beaver meadow. Brady was a fur trader in the early days; he'd settled on the upper Halfway, Cypress Creek to be exact, and had married an Indian girl named Bessie who was a daughter of Lily, then the Beaver chief.

It was winter, and Joe and I slept outdoors in our warm goose-down sleeping bags, I atop an air mattress which I'd inflated with my L.L. Bean rubber pump I still use, then let out enough air so that when I was lying on my side, my hipbone was just short of touching the icy ground beneath. Joe was in a bulkier, softer bag made by his energetic wife Claire and was using a few strewn evergreen boughs for extra padding.

At about one o'clock in the moonless darkness, nearby wolves awoke us with their wild howling. The clamor went on and on with all the din of two trains, whistles wide open, passing each other at an open road crossing.

"Must have got a moose," Joe said.

We soon drifted back to sleep. We were on our way in to Ted's. During the first daylight on the north side of the stream, perhaps a dozen yards east of the trail, we saw a large moose skeleton in what had been foot-deep snow but was now trampled to the hardness of a small skating arena. Only one bone had any meat left on it, and that Joe tossed into the sleigh for his dog, Luke.

The wise old Metecheah was chief then, and one of his slim,

dark sons was named Dennis because Dennis Murphy, who'd married Claire's sister Jessie, happened to be in the teepee at the time. I knew this Beaver later as a young man, and in fact I once bartered a brown leather bridle from him.

"Plenty big," Dennis Metecheah said the first time he saw our dog Bushman. "All same wolf."

Young Metecheah and some other Indians from the Beaver tribe rode by one day when Dennis Murphy and Ed Broulette were felling some trees. They sat on their horses, laughing and slapping their thighs.

"What's your trouble?" Murphy asked finally.

"White man work like hell," said Dennis Metecheah. "Pretty soon die."

One of his friends was a brave named Whitefish, who shunned that particular food because he regarded whitefish as brothers.

Dennis Metecheah worked as a trapper and guide. One day when I asked him how thick the sheep and goats were in his region, he cannily replied, "Plenty good fish." Another day he happened past when I was splitting chucks of lodgepole pine for firewood.

"Indian plenty strong," young Metecheah bragged. "All same white man."

I wryly extended the ax handle.

"No, no," the youth recoiled. "Indian got soft hands."

The Indians we knew all had a keen sense of humor.

"Indian now all the same white man," Pen Powell told me one of them had said to him when, driving a load of King Gething's coal up the just-opened Alaska Highway, Pen encountered the other hitch-hiking. "All time go."

"Ted Green was a prince of a fellow to be with on the trail," Claire Barkley told me recently. "When he and Joe were freighting together, Joe looked after the teams and Ted did the cooking. Ted was always singing. He had a wonderful bass voice. He got along with the Indians and treated them 100 percent.

They were always glad to see Ted and Joe coming in with fresh supplies.

"Once after a terrific wind, Lily came down from the Stoney River to cut the windfall out of the trail when he knew Ted and Joe were on their way in with a load. Another time Thomas Hunter did the same thing. When Lily died, Thomas Hunter was elected chief."

Most of the natives didn't take the fullest advantage of the stores the Indian Department gave them. Cod liver oil, for instance, was less given by the spoonful to the elders and their children than it was used to rub into saddles and harnesses.

Ted lived at what was called the Federal Ranch, built as a proposed dude ranch in 1919 by a Vancouver group. This was fronted by Captain Sam Holt, retired from the Royal Air Force, and Cap Haight. At the start, the spread had been stocked with some 140 head of Hereford cattle, driven up from Alberta.

Holt, Haight, Ted Green, Bill Carter, and Dan Macdonald had put up wild hay for them with the help of a mower and rake brought in by Del Miller by travoise. This is a primitive vehicle, in the early days more commonly used by the Plains Indians. It consists of two trailing, horse-drawn poles serving as shafts and joined by a platform for the load. That initial winter had been so severe that, finally reduced to browsing on young evergreens, all but about two dozen of the cattle had perished.

The next winter all the men managed to save was one pure-bred bull that they coddled along in the barn and fed rolled oats. When Cap Haight disappeared after shooting Guy Robison at Taylor Flats, the venture was given up. Ted took over the property for wages. When I first saw the meadows around the little group of log buildings, they were strewn with the whitened bones and skulls of dead cattle.

Joe Barkley saved Teddy Green's life one time in 50°-below-zero weather when the pair were coming down from the Stoney River with two sleighs. Joe was some distance ahead. He had his own team unhitched and a fire blazing at their camping spot when Ted pulled up. At that moment Joe was in the bush, gathering more standing dead wood for the fire.

During the process of unhitching, one of Ted's horses threw up her head, hit Ted in the face, and knocked him down. He was sprawled in the snow nearly unconscious, and if Joe hadn't happened to be there soon afterwards, Ted would undoubtedly soon have died of exposure. Ted was a small man, and Joe managed to get him to the fire and warmed up.

"With his glasses broken, he was just about helpless during the remainder of the journey," Claire told us. "Luckily, he had a spare pair at the Ranch."

Gunnar Johnson, who bred pure-blooded malemutes, later went in with Ted Green at the Federal Ranch. He was a hard-working, picturesque sourdough who retained his Scandinavian accent.

Harry Garbitt was the Indian Agent at Moberly Lake, which is just a wide spot in a river that later flows into the Peace from the south. Harry had ridden north from Edmonton years before, gathering more and more of a herd of unbranded horses as he went.

He was a sturdy, bluff Scot who handled the Cree encampment in a friendly and conscientious fashion, picked up mail and supplies at Hudson Hope, and traded his furs with the local outpost of the far-flung Hudson's Bay Company to which originally all Western Canada had been granted by the King of England. In a later struggle for the fur trade, the young and energetically daring Northwest Company, represented by such leaders as Sir Alexander Mackenzie, literally absorbed the more complacent H.B.C. in a far-reaching legal agreement that included the retention of the venerable name of the oldest trading corporation in the world.

"INCORPOPATED 2ND MAY 1670," announced in Old English lettering the sign in front of the Bay's red-roofed, white-

walled store at Hudson Hope. With a disregard for trifles befitting a concern that had been over a century old before the United States was born, no one had ever bothered to add the corrective stroke to the erroneous *P*. The sign always crowded our minds with visions of baled furs, huge freight canoes, and brightly sashed French Canadian voyageurs perspiring beneath their loads at Canada's numerous portages.

Moberly Lake was a couple of days' travel time south of Hudson Hope back then, and Harry Garbitt had a cabin on the east shore of Maurice Creek where he stayed and boiled the kettle during cold weather and warm. The only time he was unable to cross to the Hope was when ice was forming in the fall and breaking up in the spring.

When the six-miles-per-hour current was flowing in that wide part of river, any traveler from the south made his presence known by a campfire and perhaps a rifle blast. The British Columbia authorities maintained a free ferry. Fred Monteith with his sturdy rowboat was one of the early ferrymen. He was succeeded by Vic Peck who improved the situation with one of the traditionally long and heavy riverboats, powered by a so-called kicker. Billy Kruger later took over, similarly equipped but with an even larger outboard motor.

The chief of the Moberly Lake Crees for a long time was Doki who often accompanied Garbitt to Hudson Hope. Doki was a small, judicious, wizened man. No one knew his age for sure, but I saw him still going strong when it was reckoned he was 107 years old.

Harry Garbitt was also postmaster at Moberly Lake. Dealing with the families of the forest as he did, he found fur more plentiful than money. Once a cautious departmental inspector believed he'd found a shortage in the Scot's accounts.

"Nope, the stamp money is all here," Harry disagreed, waving a hand at a little heap of squirrel pelts that were held together with an elastic. "These are worth two bits apiece."

"You don't mean that you trade stamps for squirrel skins," the official said. "My gracious, I don't know what the department back in Victoria would say."

"Some Crees needed stamps," Harry explained calmly. "They didn't have any cash. Squirrel fur sells for 25 cents apiece now at the Bay. So I just took the skins instead."

| 22 |

Spring with Experience

▲

Jack Adams, slim, tall, straight, handsome prospector and ax man, came back from a dozen years of mining in Alaska and the Yukon in time to make the striking Lucile Kariel Adams his wife in 1913.

Departing from Prince George, the couple crossed the Continental Divide, left Summit Lake where they had bought land, and journeyed down the Crooked and Parsnip Rivers to Mount Selwyn, the highest peak in the Peace River mountains. On this quartz-loaded Mountain of Gold, they built a log cabin and put in the winter across from the glacier-spotted Wolverine Mountains.

The Adamses came to Selwyn as the summer-brown ptarmigan were turning white with the first snows. The mountain, they soon learned, is more than a loftiness of spruce and rock, then willow after timberline is reached. It is an immensity of glitter and shadow, basically unaltered since Mackenzie and his voyageurs poled, lined, and paddled east and then south around it. Yet Selwyn's aspect differs from hour to hour, always blending one mood with another. Its beauty moves the spirit.

"I was always somewhat psychic," Lucile maintained, "and I had the feeling that my father was beside me there on magnificent, untouched Selwyn, telling Jack and me, 'My children, buy this land, not just for a home but for an investment for yourselves and your children. A great city will grow here.'"

So they acquired some 500 acres and kept it, paying the

annual pittance of taxes until B. C. Hydro, which would have taken it anyway by eminent domain, bought it from them. All in all, Jack and Lucile secured some thousand acres along the Peace, some more of it at Wicked River, and the remainder just west of Jim Beattie's Gold Bar ranch, from which it was separated by a mountainside on whose precipitous slant were the threads of game and livestock trails.

They had boated to this latter site down the upper Peace and through the brief but dramatic white water that the sourdoughs call Parlez Pos (the rapids *qu'il ne parle pas*). These gave no warning, although later someone put up a sign on the north bank. Before that, unless he was familiar with the shoreline, a river traveler could be in their tumult before he realized it.

In the early twenties when the couple returned with two children, Jack built an elaborate home upriver of the Beattie holdings. Able to flatten a log with a broadax as if it had been planed, he constructed the house all himself. Incidentally, I found his broadax shavings the best fuel ever with which to start a fire.

Even the heavy furniture, fashioned from poles and hewn logs, was outstanding. The Adamses named their galleried home, in which there was even an organ, *All's Well*. As a result of a brief interval of friendly feuding, Jim Beattie, his pale blue eyes snapping, jovially dubbed it, *All's Hell*.

In deference to Lucile's eye for beauty, Jack put up a northern inner balcony from which depended the sleeping quarters. The edifice became the showplace of the river while it was occupied, and the Adamses cleared a flat to the west for grazing and gardening.

Mrs. Beattie still remembers Lucile politely and loudly hailing them, not wanting to surprise anyone, when she was walking over to Gold Bar, the Beatties' home, for a visit.

The Adamses, having the means, traveled for years to places like the West Indies, Mexico, and Hawaii, especially during the freezing days of winter. Then it became almost impossible to warm so high-roofed an edifice, particularly because of the picturesque if utterly impractical stone fireplace in which, this far north, the warmth of roaring logs could not even begin to keep up with the coldness transmitted by the bulk of masonry. The home was all too soon abandoned. Left unattended, the roof fell in.

Lucile always lived close to the land, searching out, cooking, and eating many edible wild plants. She was well ahead of her time in her early concern for natural foods. Lucile's favorite season remained spring. She called autumn, "merely spring with experience." In her later years she spent more and more winters in her native California and in Hawaii, even if her heart and personality never left Hudson Hope to which she always returned.

The fishing was excellent at the mouth of the stream that flowed past the Adams cabin on the east. Once Billy Kruger and I, catching a rainbow trout or Arctic grayling with a black gnat fly on at least every other cast, salted down a large washtub full which we promptly took to the Beatties, Jack and Lucile being away at the time. There at Gold Bar they were thriftily kept in the icehouse until Mrs. Beattie and the girls canned them.

On the creek by the Adamses, the scene was sequestered and peaceful. Once the three youngest Beattie children and I actually rode through a bright rainbow there, entering the prominently bended arch on our horses and finding nothing but ordinary atmosphere in the middle, then looking back to see that we had emerged on the north side of the brightly colored crescent.

The Adams spread was mainly untouched wilderness. It was different when we returned to the working ranch at Gold Bar, where Elizabeth's bright flower garden and her crab apple trees were masses of blossoms. If nurtured, fruit trees will grow in the Hudson Hope region as Elizabeth Beattie proved and Dudley

Shaw, further downriver, seconded with his and later our yearly yielding plum trees.

These latter events always occurred when autumn came around again and when up by Gold Bar everyone was pitching in with the grain harvesting. Elizabeth Beattie always retained her favorite job of stacking the mountain of sheaves, later to be pitch-forked into the rumbling line of machinery. Bundles were fed into one end, while from the other came straw, chaff that filled the air, and a golden stream of kernels which were routinely bagged and shouldered into the waiting grainery.

Even though she was a visionary, Lucile Adams was also practical. Once when she heard that I had been bemoaning the lack of yogurt in the wilderness, Lucile sent up to me with Vena the cultures of the two necessary bacteria, *Lactobacillus acidophilus* and *Streptococcus thermophilus*. Thanks to her, I was thereafter able to make the slightly acid, semifluid milk food from skimmed cow's milk, and Lucile seemed as delighted about it as I was.

Widely traveled and well educated, Lucile was a close friend of the Gething family. She was ever enthralled by new fads and was a natural advocate of Coué's, "Every day in every way I am getting better and better."

There was always a daintiness and an exquisiteness to her, and she remained alert, most interesting, and active even in her nineties. Whatever the reason, she outlived most of her doubters, remaining in good spirits and active health.

On Schooler Creek just upriver from the Adams home was another special friend, C. R. Bob Yeomans, whose main cabin and cache were neat and practical. When he wasn't in the country, there or along his strings of overnight huts, Bob was usually at the family farm at Walnut Grove. This was down the Fraser River, just east of Vancouver at the spot where we usually crossed the border.

As Canada's roads slowly improved, we made more and more trips Outside. There was always the dramatic pleasure of contrast. Too, if we stayed in the wilds too long at any one stretch we began to get "bushed." In the North country the symptoms of that include more and more of an appetite for seclusion and the increasing dislike of being interrupted by even close friends.

The first few nights away from our wilderness home were always traumatic and scary, and more than once we leaped up in fear at the sound of voices or the noise of a closing door. There was also the temporary, if no less real, initial dread of meeting new people. We both, Vena especially, needed our excursions Outside, and they ever made our overjoyed return to the solitude and seclusion all the more enticing.

At any rate, we stopped a couple of times with the hospitable Yeomans on their working farm where we enjoyed the company of Bob, his elderly and amazingly brisk mother, his cheerful and witty brother Ray, and their pretty sister Rosalie who was postmistress in Ray's country store. Once we brought Bob and his supplies back to Hudson Hope. Through his brother Ray, he was able to secure his grubstake wholesale, before he left home.

The three of us laughed together in the front seat of the heavy Packard station wagon I was driving at the time, although it wasn't so funny when a tire went flat on the then stony Hart Highway and we had to unpack the whole back of the car to get at the spare under the floor. That was the last time I carried this in its appointed place, except of course when we were driving around unloaded.

Bob Yeomans took over Charlie Jones's Carbon River trap line in 1931. He later sold this to his close friend Tommy Stott who, at one time, was a partner of Jim Beattie at Twelve Mile Ranch, a dozen miles from the start of the Portage. Tommy built a modern home there on the edge of the Peace, but unfortunately there was a mountain to the south that cut off all sunlight the year round. Tommy and his brother Henry came from Yorkshire in England. Bob originally met Tommy one harvest time in Saskatchewan.

Nearer to the Adamses, Bill Mahaffey had the Schooler Creek trap line which took in Brenham Flat. Bob later got the Schooler Creek line, as well as all the Carbon River line back from Stott.

For the pleasure of hunting and of seeing new country, I packed Bob's supplies up to the headwaters of Schooler one autumn. I got to know him even better one winter when, ill from eating spoiled moose meat, he managed to get downriver where he stayed for a few weeks to recuperate.

Bob is a medium-sized, unassuming, and quiet gentleman. There had been a dispute of long standing as to whether a particular beaver pond at the northeast corner of Brenham Flat belonged to the Schooler Creek or to the Beattie line. Soft-voiced Bob settled the matter before it reached the proportions of an open quarrel by himself trapping off all the beavers. Jim Beattie, direct and always to the point, later told me approvingly that this was indeed the best way of settling the quandary.

So passed another "spring with experience."

| *23* |

Lighter Moments

▲

BILL CARTER, the former Royal North West Mounted Police-man, was the prime prankster in Hudson Hope. There was the time when he took some dry moose droppings—about the size and shape of elongated cough drops—coated them with choco-late, and presented them to a party being held by one of the Hudson Hope women. There, the ensuing surprise and conster-nation were acute, and it was a long time before the female sector of the town eased up on him.

Actually, the moose like the rabbit is a strict vegetarian, and in the North during hard times Indians have commonly made a soup of rabbit droppings. Besides, it's a fact that Eskimos eat the contents of caribous' stomachs, which are pleasantly vine-gary like regularly served greens. But all this didn't soothe the outraged ladies.

The last time Bill Carter converted an oil drum into a heater for us, he pressed several widely assorted items into service. These included a discarded stew pot for the stove pipe collar, a damper from an old Queen Heater, a piece of scrap iron for the door catch, and the hounds of an old bobsleigh for legs. If these particular gadgets had not been on hand, it is a foregone conclu-sion that this ex-Mounted Policeman would have cheerfully substituted something else.

"All you need, Brad," Bill told me when I was writing a book about how to build log cabins, "is a cold chisel, a hammer, some odds and ends, a big chaw of tobacco, and go to work on the barrel."

It's sort of like the case of a cook on a Canadian Geographical Survey party. Dr. W. H. McLearn of Ottawa had led that group into the Peace River country one of our first summers there.

"Now where is that blasted, cussed, ding-danged. . . .?" Dr. McLearn, who's still puzzled about what was finally dished out that evening, heard this temperamental cook ranting. "Oh, to blazes with it. This will do."

At one of the early dances when more than the usual amount of liquor was being imbibed, Jack Pennington, not at all himself when under the influence, got quite unpleasant. Bill Carter and Pennington's other friends wanted to get Jack out of the way without hurting his feelings. So Bill told him that more rum was cached on the other side of the river.

Jack in his tipsy condition was soon convinced by the story and willingly went over there in search of more firewater. He was still looking when the ferry returned across the rather wide stretch of current to the Hudson Hope landing. Pennington was left all alone.

Imagine the astonishment of all when Jack Pennington, having swum the treacherous Peace in the darkness, showed up again at the dance, dripping wet.

The same Jack Pennington, once freighter on the boat called the *Ingenika,* a trapper, and a good man with a horse, was, a half century ago, widely known as Jack Lemon because of his propensity for lemon extract when nothing stronger was available. Such substitution was a common practice; some of the hardier sourdoughs even drank Sloan's liniment. The leaders of survey parties leaving the Hope usually saw to it that their supplies contained nonalcoholic vanilla and lemon flavorings. Some of the cooks handily get around this by letting portions of their purposefully accumulated dried fruit sauces ferment.

There was the forever worrying old-timer, Fred Monteith, who, when the doorway in his new privy turned out to be too narrow to accommodate his increasing bulk, solved the problem with a minimum of trouble by whittling just enough of a hollow to allow the passage of his bulging abdomen, then eased sideways in and out of the Chic Sales.

Lord and Lady Willingdon, when the former was the Governor General of Canada, arrived aboard the *D. A. Thomas* on an unscheduled trip to Hudson Hope one morning when Wes and Jean Gething happened to be down at the landing. The visitors had heard of the Gethings through Lord Rhondda, who also had local coal holdings, so the four immediately struck up an acquaintance and walked up the hill together. Later the two ladies journeyed across the Portage together in a ramshackle automobile that had been brought in by river, there then being no road to the Outside.

There was no road across the Portage either, and it took the effort of all the sourdoughs present to push the car through the cemetery to the flat above. Then on the way to the head of Rocky Mountain Canyon something went wrong with the motor. This was eventually repaired on the spot with one of Lady Willingdon's hairpins. Afterwards, when several times the car hit a really severe bump, the wife of the Governor General exclaimed, "Oops, my hairpin!" This became a catch phrase in Hudson Hope.

Joe Gilmette homesteaded across river in 1912 or so. He cleared and worked land clad only in Stanfield underwear, in his bare feet even though troubled by yellow jackets which nested in the ground. Although he often labored in no clothes at all, he had a clean suit of long johns for formal attire. Joe left Hudson Hope after a short, memorable interval.

Bill Innis, homesteader who located on the Red River in 1916, bringing in cattle and horses and trading and trapping in addition to ranching, eventually sold out to Bill Erb who had ridden a saddle horse up from the States. Erb was called Dried Apples Erb because he lived on water and this dried fruit.

A stopping place on the Alaska Highway that was known as Lum 'n' Abner's, whose coffee shop burned down in 1963, used a catchy slogan that's the envy of Madison Avenue: "Fill your tank and tummy, too: at Mile Two Hundred and Thirty-Two."

There was the time that some notables from Victoria visited Wes and Jean Gething at their sawmill just below the Portage on Beryl Prairie. Although Jean was doing the cooking, the mill didn't have an actual cookhouse. So there were more than a dozen present with dinnertime coming up. Jean was perplexed about how in the world she was going to feed that many. Then a friend of theirs happened along with a big batch of bear steaks. She broiled these.

In the midst of the meal, one of the gentlemen from Victoria inquired, "What kind of meat is this?"

"Venison," Wes said promptly.

The other replied, "Oh, that's good. I thought it might be bear steak. I can't be fooled on bear. I wouldn't eat bear meat for anything."

"Of course, we had to struggle to keep our faces very straight," Jean told me later. "If we had told him the truth, he'd have gone outside and been sick."

Such an incident actually happened at King Gething's older coal mine one noon when the long table was crowded with miners and truckers. A beef-like aroma filled the cookshack, for Kay Ohland had been making a mulligan from a bear I'd harvested. Milton Vince, one of the truckers, reached for a hearty third serving.

Afraid that Scotty and I, who were to be alone there over the weekend, wouldn't have enough left to eat, Mrs. Ohland finally asked with an air of innocence, "How do you like the bear meat, Milton?"

"Bear!" young Vince exclaimed.

He was seated next to the door, and he hurried outside where we heard the sounds of retching.

Once a prankster, who turned out to be Mrs. Harry Barr, put a skunk skin under Jim Ruxton's pillow during his bachelor days. Jim finally asked Wes and Jean Gething to help him locate the source of the awful stench. It was they who discovered the source.

It reminded Jean of an opening day at one of the many schools at which she taught. A frightful odor permeated the place. Finally, two boys admitted killing a skunk a fortnight previously and, in self-defense, burying all their clothes except the rubber shoes they were still wearing. These they had repeatedly scoured and scrubbed. Yet a half month later the rubber retained enough of the skunk perfume to drive everyone from the building to a class outdoors. Even if they'd known of the efficacy of tomato juice to destroy skunk odor, there was none of it around.

Once Jean and a small party of women stopped at Ed Rushton's cabin, Happy Valley, near the MacDougall place at the mouth of Lynx Creek a few miles downstream from Hudson Hope. Ed was rightfully famous for his pies. He hospitably cut huge hunks for each visitor and handed them big kitchen knives, with blades about an inch wide and nine or ten inches long. Ed had forks, but in his etiquette book knives were the implements with which to dine on pie.

Jean had her three-year-old Beryl with her, so she asked for a spoon with which to feed the infant. She found one, luckily. But she'll never forget Edith Kyllo, who was with the group, looking helpless but managing.

The good-natured sourdoughs, a few in particular, were always on the outlook for tricks to play on one another. One memorable incident is credited to Charlie Paquette.

Charlie had a small cabin handily below the great spring in

Hudson Hope. Once while Charlie had been away, a social group of wasps started a nest under the seat of his privy. Charlie decided to leave it intact for the proper moment.

Sure enough, some neighbors soon descended on his place for a session of poker. It wasn't until one of them had to make use of the facilities that Charlie informed the others, safe behind the cabin window, about what to expect.

A few moments later there was an outburst of pained curses. The victim stumbled into sight, trying to escape the stinging insects and tripping over his half-lowered trousers. When it was over, he was greeted with robust merriment in which he soon joined.

Jack Pennington had the Clearwater River trap line when Bob Yeomans first came to Hudson Hope. Leo Rutledge later trapped the Clearwater in the middle of the Rockies, several years teaming up successfully with Bobby Beattie in this magnificent part of the Peace River country. Leo afterwards sold to Jack Longstreet.

Jack Longstreet, who was a large and not bad-looking sourdough, was for some reason—cabin fever probably—deathly afraid of women. When he heard any feminine voice up by his Clearwater cabin he would go into the woods and hide.

Vena, not knowing of Jack's dread, was gleefully introduced to Longstreet one afternoon in the Hudson's Bay Company store. As she companionably and unsuspectingly approached Jack, attempting to strike up a conversation, that worthy kept retreating until, nearly cornered, he finally made his escape out the back door. It wasn't until later, amid peals of laughter, that she found out what had been the trouble.

When King Gething moved his coal operations about a mile to a new eight-and-one-half-foot seam of bituminous, his old cabins were left vacant. Jack, alone and more bushed than ever, happily took over on the soon overgrown spur road.

Wingy Robinson came in from the town of Peace River about

1915 and built a little cabin in the bush on Bull Creek. Even in this land of singular and self-sufficient individuals he was regarded as a character, a role he accented with his bouts with booze.

The Hudson Hope mail used to come in from Fort St. John by pack horse or sleigh when the Peace was icebound, by river the rest of the year. Since there were no liquor stores nearer, the old-timers had to send out by mail to Pouce Coupe, below Dawson Creek near the Alberta border, for their overproof Hudson's Bay Company rum or for whatever else was their fancy of the moment. One Christmas season they'd planned to be particularly merry a few of the old boys were heartbroken to receive only broken bottles.

That part of the mail came in heavy, padlocked canvas sacks. What happened was that this holiday season had been particularly cold. The mail carrier, making a frosty camp by the trail, had thoughtfully suspended one of the gurgling sacks from a tree limb, put a galvanized pail beneath, and belabored the thick canvas with a club until enough of the ardent spirits seeped into the waiting bucket to improve his outlook on life. The few unhappy customers were later recompensed by the government liquor store because the result of the undiscovered maneuver was regarded as merely another routine incident of mail being damaged in shipment.

Cheechakos furnished much humor, among them the tenderfoot who seriously inquired of Jim Holden, H.B.C. manager at the time, "Which is warmer, sir? Snowshoes or moccasins?"

Another wilderness amateur, during one of our absences, built his fire in the oven of our large black stove, evidently not realizing there is such a refinement as a firebox.

Sourdoughs themselves also set the stage for many a guffaw. Where but in the Farther Places, for example, would one appreciate someone like the cheerful Scotty Smith?

"I can stick needles through my cheeks," the athletic young

Scot was boasting good-humoredly one day. He was entertaining a group waiting in the Hudson Hope post office while Vesta Gething was putting up the latest shipment of mail. "Doesn't bother me a bit."

"That's right," King Gething agreed, "but you can't stand to have me put iodine on a cut."

Then there was the prospector on the upper Peace, Mulligan Jones, who, according to Dudley Shaw, slept with his head in a mulligan bucket after someone had informed him that hungry pack rats sometimes nip a slumberer's ears. This wasn't as far-fetched as one might suppose; Jean Gething once awoke to find a pack rat nibbling her hair.

Legend records the occasion when the same Dudley Shaw brewed a decoction of juniper berries for an ailing schoolmaster who was boarding with him. In the dimness of the small-windowed cabin, the teacher mistakenly grasped and drank a pan of dishwater, made a hurried trip outdoors, and although never the wiser was cured, anyway.

Scotty, with his inherent thrift, had an ingenious way of prolonging the life of a pair of socks. First of all, he would wear them the ordinary way. When they developed holes in the heels, he'd turn them over and don them in that fashion. Then there was each of the two sides. If the hosiery was long enough, the Edinburgh lad would finally cut off the offending stocking feet, tie the open ends, and go through the whole procedure again. When he could, he'd have long woolen tubes knitted for his prolonged use in this fashion.

Vena and I got our fresh eggs from Matt and Erna Boe who generally left them with Vesta Gething at the post office. One frigid winter day I went in to pick up our weekly mail. Vesta, handing it over with her usual smile, apologized, "Erna says she's sorry, but there are no eggs this week. It's been so cold that the hens have stopped laying."

Piped up Dudley Shaw behind me, to a roar of merriment, "I don't blame them."

Hudson Hope animals also develop personalities. One dog, when he wanted to come into the cabin during especially cold spells, used to appear at the door and whine, with a stick of firewood irresistibly between his jaws.

A white cat at King Gething's coal mine became as dark as a marten when left alone for long, as occasionally happened when the operation was closed down for a few months. The brief appearance of human beings made no apparent difference in the cat's toilet. But when a person stayed as long as three days, the feline figured that the visit was going to be more permanent and began to polish up.

Cloud, Vena's gray gelding, was the only cayuse I have ever encountered who had no sense of direction. Everyone who has ridden knows that it is a natural state of affairs for a horse to be livelier and more eager when on the way home. But I could spend a day hunting with Cloud who, unlike my less placid Chinook, would not spook when I shot while still astride; I could take him for a drink at the runoff a few yards up the main trail from where I usually emerged from the bush, and then he'd hasten with equal ardor whether I turned him upriver or down toward his corral and oat sheaves.

Chinook, more characteristically, kept slyly and slowly turning in a wide circle toward our cabin unless I kept close tabs by sun or compass when I was hunting with her in the thick bush.

There was a bearberry bush outside our southern expanse of windows that Vena kept full of cookies, suet, bread, and other tidbits for the smaller forest folk. Besides the gray Canada jays and the snowbirds whose plumage turned from brown to white in winter, there were two main visitors. One was Sammy the Squirrel. The other was a slim, sleek creature who was Willie the Weasel during the warm weather and, when the snow came and his fur became sheer white except for a tiny black tail tip, Herman the Ermine.

That small animal, a fascinating if bloodthirsty little beast, particularly liked the chunks of fresh red moose meat that I nailed to the wooden ledge outside the glass so that he would eat on the spot. He became so tame that I could come to within three-and-one-half feet of him, the normal focal length of my Leica lens, to snap his picture.

Both squirrel and weasel vied for the dainties on the bush, the slim Willie appearing unexpectedly from burrows beneath the snow, then slithering back as rapidly. For its size, the weasel is among the most menacing animals of the woods, and it never failed to astonish us that the less savagely equipped squirrel could chase it all over the yard.

At first Vena used to suspend the victuals from the bush with string. One offering was a dense, heavy loaf of sourdough bread which had unexpectedly failed to rise and which, although it was still edible, we made a gift of to our hungrier neighbors. As did the weasel, the red squirrel liked to cache a food supply. Sammy gnawed and chawed at the bit of twine until, abruptly, we saw the whole thing give way and fall with a thud that could have seriously injured Sammy if he had been under it. From that day on, our lesson learned, we used wire.

We found Sammy particularly liked raw rolled oats, and afterwards there was always a little saucer of cereal awaiting him mornings on the otherwise fossil-filled window ledge.

During the cold dark nights of the northern winter we kept no overnight fire, relying instead on our warm 90x90 white goose-down sleeping bags which we spread out in the northwest corner of our cabin on a bunk of flat lumber, under which we stored such things as duffle bags and firewood. When the temperature fell as much as the common 30° below zero Fahrenheit, Vena preferred to drowse mornings in the luxury of her sleeping robe.

On the other hand, I liked an early breakfast. This problem we solved handily to the complete satisfaction of us both.

At night I used to let the fire in the cookstove, within arm's length of my side of the bunk, go out early. Then, as soon as the metal had cooled, I would lay in the next morning's fire makings of fuzzsticks—slim sticks of straight-grained lodgepole pine which I shaved again and again with my Randall hunting knife until they became masses of resinous curls—then small dry kindling, and finally a few heavier pieces of softwood.

The next morning a long wooden kitchen match, lit from my bed and dropped into the awaiting fire makings, generally started a blaze roaring at the first try. Later I'd feed it, still without quitting my sanctuary, with nearby chunks of split pine. In fact, the only time I left my sleeping bag was to dash barefooted over to my working corner and turn on our battery-powered Zenith portable radio, already tuned to Al Cummings, Seattle disk jockey, whose chatter we found entertaining.

I'd have my own portion of rolled oats, raisins, salt, and water already atop the stove. When this started to plop, I'd transfer the pan to the bookstand at the head of the bunk, drop in a quickly melting slab of margarine, and enjoy my morning repast. In other words, I'd cook my own breakfast each morning without bothering the drowsing Vena.

But let the red squirrel finish his meal, especially during the intense cold when he was especially ravenous, and he'd start scratching on the windowpane for more. The kind-hearted Vena would hear this at once and, leaving her goose down, dart to the door and replenish the supply. I beat her to it a few times, of course, and Sammy was so enthusiastic that his cold little feet sought my hand as I was pouring more oats into his dish.

This was all fine, and I didn't mind at all, especially as the sun does not rise until about ten o'clock during the shorter days of winter. I do not like to write under even the bright artificial light of our Coleman gasoline-fueled lantern unless a deadline looms. So there was usually plenty of time for the cabin to warm before we dressed for the day.

But word of the practice got around the village, and it became a standing joke that Vena would get up to feed a hungry squirrel but not her hungry husband.

| 24 |

Social Butterfly and Others

▲

IF HUDSON HOPE could have been said to have a social butterfly, it was Edith McFarland. Dudley Shaw, who was an
honored guest at many of her teas, had affectionately dubbed
her Aunty Mac, and the name stuck. When we knew her first,
she was taking care of the home of Fred Gaylor, the town
telegrapher across the road from the Bay, and living nearby in
her own neat and sunny cabin with her young daughter
Beverly.

Tall Joe McFarland, who had been trapping and homesteading on the upper reaches of the Halfway River since 1919,
brought Edith to the wilderness directly from the busy seaport
of Vancouver. Joe, who had invented a device long used on
many traps, was one of the finest and most meticulous log
craftsmen I have ever known; Jack Adams was the other one. It
was Joe who built the log Hudson Hope Hotel for Bob and
Maude Ferguson.

Joe took Edith, who'd been terrified of the curious if friendly
Beaver Indians on the Halfway, to Hudson Hope in 1920. They
homesteaded on the north bank of the Peace, nearly five miles
up Rocky Mountain Canyon, where a small stream from which
they got their water cascaded into the river some 60 feet below.
This little brook was variously known as Portage Creek and
Four Mile Creek, both names assigned it because of the way it
crossed the Portage four miles upstream of the Hope.

The quarter section the McFarlands proved up was directly east of our own homesite which straddled the clearer and narrower Bull Creek. This got its start north-northwest of its own taller waterfall that splashed onto a reef. The flow came from the eastern side of Bullhead Mountain, several miles inland through a spruce and poplar forest where the moose, deer, and bear hunting was excellent. The McFarlands had already moved next to the church and the fenced H.B.C. compound, just down the road from town, by the time we arrived.

Edith became the social leader in the Hope and supervised many a bridge party and church social. When Fred Gaylor was transferred to Fort St. John in 1941 and later to Dawson Creek, the telegraph key was replaced by a crank telephone, and Edith McFarland took over the duties in her own bright home.

The copper wire to Fort St. John tied in with Edmonton and thus the outside world. Because of the way it had been strung beside the trail downriver, it was very vulnerable, largely because of falling timber. Maintaining the connection necessitated long and many times frosty patrols. Because it was the only link with the Outside at a time when it sometimes took several days to reach Fort St. John, Fred and Gladys Gaylor, who assumed responsibility for its operations in the early 1920s, became very important members of the community.

For a long period Kathy Peck—who'd trained as a nurse in England before moving to Hudson Hope with saddle and pack horses in 1923, and who was long the only nurse in town—got medical advice on some of her problems from doctors in Fort St. John. Later Marion Cuthill, hospital nurse who met the local H.B.C. factor as the result of his motorcycle accident and had married him, helped Kathleen. Not long afterward, the Red Cross established an outpost at the Hope with rotating nurses, pepping up the bachelors.

One Sunday afternoon Vena had scheduled a meeting of the

informal bridge club at our cabin, but it had rained in the meantime, making the trail heavy with mire. Vena had just about given up hope when there was a hearty hail from Edith and her little group, "Here we come, Vena." I had just enough time to escape for a day of hunting upriver. My lunch had been packed just in case the ladies should make it through.

Edith or "Aunty Mac" was a supreme hostess, and there was many a delicious meal Vena, Dudley, I, and usually a few others enjoyed in her comfortable home at the bottom of the hill descending into the small settlement. One spring I was so busy in trying to meet a deadline on a book that I couldn't take the time to attend one of the community dances. The ladies of the town were donating sandwiches, cookies, pies, cakes, and other homemade fare to the function which promised to be such fun that I didn't want Vena to miss it.

So Vena put her finery in Cloud's saddle bags, dressed for the occasion at Aunty Mac's, and attended the event with Beverly. Afterwards she changed back into her woods attire at the McFarlands, restoring the other garb to the saddle bags, and rode back home where I was glad to see her. She was bubbling with enthusiasm partly because, as she had danced in ballet and in stage shows ever since she'd been a small girl, she was a much sought partner.

Nearly every sourdough, perhaps because of the silent and sure way they had learned to make their way through the forest, had a superb sense of rhythm and danced with fervor, a few of the taller of them actually twirling her through the air on some of the turns.

I'll never forget the get-acquainted dance that the sourdoughs rigged up in our honor when we first came to the Hope. It was Dudley Shaw, on a trip around his trap line, who told us about it. Bob Yeomans who trapped some 50 miles away on Schooler Creek attended, having heard of the occasion by what is known as *moccasin telegraph,* the slightly incredible way in which information is exchanged through the nearly vacant wilds.

Again, the dance was put on in the large hewn-log restaurant of the Boyntons, and Ted and Ivy kept a huge pot of coffee on the back of the stove. Local families provided pot luck. Marvelle Murphy and Ruth Blair vied with one another in making an accordion sound like an orchestra.

The thirty folks present were happy, good-natured, and hearty, and they were quick to introduce themselves. There were the usual fox-trots, waltzes, and polkas. Everyone had such a splendid time that the party didn't break up until the early morning.

We became acquainted with a large percentage of Hudson Hope's population that night, and most of them became close friends. Here, where people were so scarce, everyone was dependent on each other. Friendships really meant a great deal.

It isn't just taking care of someone in trouble. Mere acquaintances will do that much as a matter of course. For instance, Jim Beattie and neighboring Dick Hamilton, after some long-forgotten dispute, had not spoken to each other for years. Yet when Dick fell seriously ill, it was Jim who took him the 80 miles to the hospital in Fort St. John. Here when an individual hears of a friend in difficulty, he doesn't inquire, "What can I do?" He only wants an answer to, "Where is he?"

One chinooking winter day Dave Cuthill, his wife Marion, and I set out for Fort St. John, Dawson Creek, and Pouce Coupe in the Hudson Bay factor's sedan. The night when we returned, after a convivial supper in Fort St. John at Judge Ray Sandy's, it was freezing. The trail was icy. Despite several tries, we were unable to get up the steep hill at Farrell Creek. We had to turn back and seek shelter at Dan and Dorothy Macdonald's.

Some of the family of mostly girls were kind enough to bunk double so as to make room for the three of us. I recall that the children, hungry for company, could hardly wait for us to get up the next morning. They were whispering by my couch in the main room, "Is he still asleep? Yes, he's still asleep."

After a bountiful breakfast, Dave and I left Marion in the comfortably warm cabin and hiked toward Hudson Hope for transportation. It was a crisp and beautiful morning, and from the top of one of the more formidable of the inclines, we heard coyotes and saw their dark forms on the frozen river below. Not far away Myrtle Robison was filling a couple of buckets from a hole Guy had earlier chopped in the ice and covered with spruce boughs.

Dave and I had tea at the Robisons', where Guy insisted that I accept as a present an Indian-beaded moosehide knife sheath I'd admired. Then we continued our stroll to Hudson Hope where we got Ted Boynton to go back to Dan's and Dorothy's for Marion, the car, and the supplies we had picked up on our trip out.

Dan was a rugged, powerful (what was locally known as *skookum),* black-haired Scot. He was so husky that he once toted over the Portage, without noticing the difference, an already heavy packsack into whose empty spaces prankster Bill Carter had loaded rocks. Dan had come from the Orkneys, islands off northern Scotland where he was a fisherman. In his early days he used to get away in his dory so early in the morning that his usual breakfast consisted of handfuls of rolled oats wadded in his right hand and dipped into the brine to moisten and flavor them.

Dan Macdonald came into the region soon after 1910, when he helped build the Grand Trunk Railroad to Prince George. Afterwards, he and Jack Thomas felt the call of the Peace River country. The usual way in from the west was by boat, but both were bringing horses, Dan half a dozen and Jack only one.

The dim trail through Pine Pass was interlaced with alluring game trails, and after frequent disputes over which route to follow, each man finally went his own way. Dan reached the Clearwater River where it mingled with the Peace from the south. One of his cayuses unfortunately broke a leg and had to be shot, so Dan made the horse part of his grub supply.

Jack, too, ran short of food and for meat had to put a bullet into the brain of his one horse. Gradually becoming weaker and weaker and able to pack less and less of the too lean meat, he was almost starved by the time he came to the mouth of the Pine River. Here he was found by Frank Beaton, then the H.B.C. manager, who took him to the post where, with Jack close to death, Mrs. Beaton fed and cared for him until, gratefully, he was robust enough to build a cabin and barn on the land they had bought in Hudson Hope.

In the meantime Dan Macdonald homesteaded on Farrell Creek on the downriver side of the Hump, left awhile to fight in World War I with the Canadian Army, and got back in time to go with Jim Beattie and a constable from Fort St. John to investigate an Indian report of the murders of "two crazy white men" at a lake up the Sikanni River.

Jack Thomas had packed in the pair with their supplies and grubstake. Jack affirmed that the duo had bickered throughout the trip and were still quarreling when he left, having accomplished all he had been hired to do. The best way that Dan, Jim, and the constable could reconstruct the crime was that the Mexican had shot the American, after which the Texan had returned a deadly shot through the heart. That gave the body of water its name, Deadman Lake.

A bit downriver from Dan's ranch lived Teddy Yates, jolly little Devonshireman, who came to the Hudson Hope area from Saskatchewan during the first years of the depression. Then in the Peace River country a thrifty bachelor could homestead and live well on less than five dollars a week, buying little but flour, sugar, tea, milk, and baking powder. This meant he'd be using wild meat, lard rendered from the fat of the plentiful black bears (the best ever for such things as flaky pie crust), wild berries, his choice of the numerous edible wild plants, plus the harvest of an abundant garden. Teddy was long on the latter; for years he supplied the Hudson Hope merchants and some of the settlers with produce delivered with his familiar pickup truck.

Teddy had been one of the early homesteaders on Beryl Prairie, later working for Phil Tompkins downriver at the latter's sawmill and finally settling at Bear Flat between the Hope and Fort St. John. Here his good friend Les Bazeley, who for years carried the mail to and from Hudson Hope, obliged him by swapping a plot of particularly fertile riverside land for Teddy's proved-up quarter section across the road. In Yates's vegetable garden produce grew to amazing sizes in the spring and summer, with care, weeding, fertilizing, watering, and some twenty hours of daylight. The weeks when the sun is at its highest you can comfortably read a newspaper outdoors at midnight in Hudson Hope.

Although he had an aversion to talking about it, Teddy Yates had a scarred hand as a result of a First World War shelling. Unlike most other upper Peace River veterans such as Dan, he did not belong to the Legion.

Dan was trapping at every opportunity, and he was so strong that when the heavy Bill Keily was stricken with appendicitis while Macdonald was running a trap line with him during the winter of 1922-1923, Dan by himself pulled the critically ill Keily to where the latter could get the medical attention that saved his life.

Dan's union with the cheerful and competent Dorothy Passmore a few years later soon made him the father of a family large enough to warrant a special schoolhouse nearby. Alice Tompkins and later Dorothy herself, a former schoolmarm, were among the teachers. It was Dan's ambition at this time to man the Hudson Hope ferry, but Vic Peck was ably holding down that job.

Later Dorothy was able to talk Dan into moving to the coast. There the girls and Dan, Jr. would no longer have to do heavy ranch work, and they could get a better education. Aunty Mac told us about seeing Dan Macdonald in the capital city of Victoria, elegant and proudly straight as a Commissionaire at the British Columbia Parliament Buildings.

| *25* |

Royal North West Mounted Policeman

▲

Ex-Constable William Harold Carter, for years one of the most famous sourdoughs of Hudson Hope, was born in England. He joined the Regimental North West Mounted Police on November 25, 1903 at the age of 21 years and 11 months. According to the records now stored by the present Royal Canadian Mounted Police in Ottawa, Bill at that time was five feet and seven and three-quarters inches tall, weighed 147 pounds, and had brown hair, blue eyes, and a fair complexion. Constable Carter listed his previous occupation as that of a stud groom in England, his previous residence as Winnipeg.

Bill served in Regina until 1905 when, according to the official archives, he was transfered to N Division. He then spent nearly three years working on the proposed Peace-Yukon Trail through the wilderness that passed near Hudson Hope where he was to stake land in 1912. After three hard years of trail slashing, he returned to Calgary in the latter part of 1907.

"Constable Carter took his discharge from the Force on November 24, 1908," state the officials of the colorful Police. "He retired to Hudson Hope."

On the first of March during 1905 a new R.N.W.M.P. division, designated N, was organized to "open up a pack trail from Fort St. John, B.C., to Teslin Lake, Yukon Territory, across the mountains of British Columbia. Superintendent Charles Constantine was appointed to the command. He reported:

"A detachment of two officers, thirty noncommissioned officers and constables, and sixty horses left Fort Saskatchewan on March 17 for this work. Owing to the breaking up of the winter roads, the journey was very trying, but they reached Peace River Crossing, 350 miles from Fort Saskatchewan, on April 9 without any serious mishap. Here they were delayed, awaiting supplies, until May 21 when the party left for Fort St. John, arriving there June 1."

Bill Carter, young and robust and excited, was then near Hudson Hope which he would soon enrich with his permanent presence. He was a prankster even in those early days, and over tea in the Gething kitchen and at both King's and Lloyd's mines he often chuckled while telling me of his always good-natured mischief. That very special kind of chocolate candy he brought to a local ladies' party was just one example.

"Work commenced on the Trail on June 15 and was suspended on September 25, owing to heavy snow in the mountains. Ninety-four miles of trail were completed. It was expected that more progress would have been made, but unforeseen difficulties were encountered in unfordable streams which had to be bridged, steep banks which had to be graded, and extensive windfalls through which the trail had to be literally sawn.

"From information we now have, we know that the heaviest work has been encountered and more rapid progress is expected after the Rocky Mountains have been crossed. Supplies for next season have been forwarded to Fort Graham, and those required for the work to that post are being pushed forward this winter by sled to the end of the Trail."

Official instructions were: "The Trail to be constructed is to be one suitable for pack animals. In selecting the location, you should bear in mind that at some future time it may be made into a wagon road. Through timber the Trail shall be eight feet wide. All boggy and soft places should be brushed, and where possible small streams should be bridged.

"The Trail is to be clearly marked, so that it can be followed by any traveller without a guide. In open country large posts should be marked with the distances in miles from Fort St. John. The numbers should be burned in so that they can not be easily erased. Rest houses are to be built every thirty miles, or at such distances as are most convenient for camping, where water and wood are easily obtainable."

Bill and his comrades soon found that the route from Fort St. John to Fort Graham, where there was an H.B.C. post, had been seldom if ever used since the Klondike gold rush seven years before. Fort Graham was much more easily reached from the East by going upriver to Hudson Hope, crossing the Portage, and then cruising up the placid Peace and afterwards up the Finlay River. They learned, too, that instead of becoming better, the further they went "the worse became the country."

The annual report of Superintendent Charles Constantine concerning the proposed Peace River-Yukon Trail for the work year ending October 31, 1906 spoke of 63°-below-zero weather during the winter just past. It also mentioned Hudson Hope.

"Before leaving Edmonton I had made arrangements with the general manager of Revillon Bros., Ltd. (our contractors) to make a trip to Fort Graham together, as there were a lot of spoiled stores to be gone over together, both at St. John and at Hudson's Hope. So I stayed at Lesser Slave lake until the arrival of this gentleman and we made the trip to St. John, arriving at that place on August 5. Here, according to Revillon's arrangements, a crew was to be awaiting our arrival to track us up the river to Graham.

"The crew, however, was found to have deserted except two, who I therefore engaged to track me in a canoe as far as Hudson's Hope where I expected to meet a hired pack train to take me over the Portage. I duly arrived at Hudson's Hope and after waiting there for two days was obliged to turn back, no means arriving to take my outfit over the Portage.

"I soon got back to Fort St. John (the stream being very swift here) when I set to work to try and hire sufficient pack horses to reach the trail party. In this I failed, as I refused to pay the sum asked ($500). There was nothing then left for me to do except to return to Peace River Crossing, which I did, arriving there on August 24, 1906. I was enabled on the trip to go over all the spoilt stores at St. John, to which point the party had cut last September.

"The 'Winter Cache' of supplies, which as before stated had been brought up from Fort St. John earlier in the year over the ice up the Half-way river, was about one mile distant from this spot. The Half-way river at this point is a considerable stream about 200 yards across. No difficulty, however, was experienced in getting across, there being two good sized sand bars in the middle of the stream. The country here is fairly open, being of the nature of flats of considerable area.

"The entire party assembled at the 'Winter Cache' which I will call Cache 1, and moved it to a point some six miles up, recrossing the stream and making a fresh Cache No. 2. A rest house was built here not far from camp 19 at 97-mile post. The country as far as the second crossing at the Half-way river lies through willow, scrub, poplar and spruce with some swampy ground interspersed by small creeks, two of which the trail crosses, then through some heavy spruce out into an open pasture interspersed with small poplar bluffs. The feed and water here are excellent. . . .

"Camp 25 was pitched about the 126 mile post in country covered by intermittent willow scrub and spruce bluffs. Just previous, the north fork of the Cypress is crossed, being 15 feet wide. Just above here there are some small falls on the Cypress river which we past on the left, going ahead to the 133 mile post. All along here we have been gradually on the assent to the summit of the Laurier pass which is reached at mile post 139 where the Cypress river has its source. . . .

"After crossing the Oscipa, which is a considerable stream 200 yards across, the trail commences to ascend to the summit of Herchmer pass where we pitched our 32nd camp."

Before this river was reached, three constables were sent ahead to Fort Graham with instructions to Corporal McLeod to commence putting up hay for the winter that comes early in these mountains. Fort Graham was reached by the main party on August 11. Revillon's scow arrived at Fort Graham, bringing up a large quantity of supplies of all sorts. Upon inspection, however, it was found that a considerable amount was spoiled, partly because of a swamping in the Ne Parle Pas Rapids. And canned butter, for example, was tainted because of nails having pierced the containers.

A small party was sent across the Finlay River with Corporal Lukey to commence the trail that was to be slashed to the famous Telegraph Trail from British Columbia and the Outside, cut earlier for a proposed telegraph line across Alaska to Siberia and on to Europe. Many prospectors had found gold in and around the Ingenika River and throughout all this country.

The police, after hacking another 20 miles through rough and rocky country to Whitefish Lakes, followed the Telegraph Trail for a ways, then returned to their caches of food and hay at Fort Graham. There William Fox, who was half Indian, was manager of the H.B.C. post near where the R.N.W.M.P. finished putting up their own quarters. The barracks measured 30 by 40 feet, while the mess room and kitchen combined were smaller.

Superintendent Charles Constantine reported that the country was extremely rough and that the work was constantly slowed by great jackpots of fallen timber, the result of fires. He told of moose, caribou, mountain sheep and goats, and bears being plentiful in the mountains. Partridge and prairie chicken were also frequently seen. The most common fur-bearing animals were lynx and marten. That winter was exceptionally mild; only five feet of snow fell and much of that was eaten away by chinooks. The low point on the thermometer was 40° below zero.

The following year the Police aborted their earlier plans and journeyed in Indian canoes down the Skeena River, reaching Port Essington on the Pacific Ocean on October 9. There they boarded the S. S. *Princess Beatrice,* arriving in Vancouver at 9 o'clock on the morning of October 14. They came to Calgary two days later.

Inspector A. E. C. McDonnell, commanding the Peace River-Yukon Trail party, reported that prospectors were sluicing 100 dollars a day each in coarse gold on bars of the Ingenika River and that gold had also been found on the upper Finlay.

After mustering out of the R.N.W.M.P. when his five-year enlistment came to an end, Bill Carter worked at odd jobs and did some trapping and prospecting until, with Fred Monteith, he came in 1912 to stake land in Hudson Hope where the wolf willow was yellow and fragrant.

Building his own cabin a short distance southwest of the friendly Gethings, from whose well he long got his water, Bill helped others put up cabins, worked at getting in wood for some of his neighbors, and occupied himself at odd jobs rather than engaging in ranching. He made rugged if somewhat crude furniture which was all the more picturesque for this, worked at Wes Gething's sawmill, and trapped on Beryl Prairie.

He also became renowned as the settlement's dentist, usually relying on overproof rum to deaden the pain of his pliers. A visiting dentist later mailed him forceps which he utilized until the Red Cross set up a small emergency clinic in quarters sold them by outfitter and trapper Leo Rutledge. Bill then gave the implement to the nurse and resigned from his profession, which had saved many a lot of suffering.

A handyman and self-styled wood butcher, he achieved even more fame as a builder of heaters from the large, readily available gasoline and coal oil drums, chiseling out doors and drafts, as well as vents for the stovepipes, and silvering the more fancy of his efforts with aluminum paint. Set on their sides on makeshift iron supports over fireproof metal or asbestos mats, these heaters could accept large chunks of wood. Bill's contraptions heated many a cabin in the area.

Prospecting became one of his sidelines, and he discovered coal on the eastern side of the Butler Range. Bill also located iron outcroppings in which he could never interest prospective developers, as at that time they were deemed not to be sufficiently extensive.

Carter, the Gethings, and trapper Stanley Wallace prospected a lot together, but as Neil Gething tried to explain to Bill, most of the latter's findings, if seemingly promising, were valueless; they were merely rocks strewn by an early glacier, not lode ore.

"I rode to British Columbia from the States at the age of 18," Stan Wallace told me, "coming down the Peace River to Hudson Hope in 1913."

Wallace was a highly independent man and did not usually join the rush of trappers to get in first with their furs in the spring in an effort to obtain the best prices. Stan arrived with his catch when it suited him. His friends frequently became concerned because Stan was late. Only once, however, did they make the error of putting together a searching party. The fiercely self-sufficient sourdough made it plain that he could take care of himself. Neither was he lonely even though, unlike most trappers, he wasn't accompanied by a dog.

The only thing that bothered Stan was that in later years he became increasingly deaf as a result of an explosion in the original coal mine on the river. Once, not equipped with a flashlight when he was exploring the dark recesses with Neil Gething, he made the mistake of lighting a match. The incident was singular for, because of the formation, gas almost never accumulates along the Peace River coal seams.

Stan's crony Bill Carter had been a friend of Staff Sergeant K. F. Anderson and had been the last prison guard of Charles King. This individual had been convicted and sentenced to death for the murder of Edward Hayward at Lesser Slave Lake on September 17, 1904, a crime solved by Anderson.

Two partners, according to the official report of Inspector D. A. E. Strickland of the Mounties, "started from Edmonton in August with an outfit of pack horses, traps, etc. for a season's hunting and trapping, going over the Swan Lake trail to Lesser Slave Lake where they were seen to arrive by a large number of Indians, whites, and breeds. They encamped on the reserve at Sucker creek, and were visited by the Indians and others. On the second day after they arrived Hayward was missing. King, with all the outfit, struck camp and moved away, saying that his partner had gone to Sturgeon Lake.

"This aroused the suspicions of the Chief, Moostoos, as a shot had been heard, and the action of King in building a huge fire on the spot, and his story about Hayward (as he had not been seen) being most improbable. Moostoos informed the R.N.W.M.P. with the result that portions of the supposed murdered man had been found in the campfire, and articles belonging to him in a slough nearby.

"The beginning of the investigation which finally led to the condemnation of King was when an Indian lad on the reserve noticed that the 'white man's dog would not follow him,' and spoke of it to the other members of the tribe. . . . It was then owing to the indefatigable work of Sergeant Anderson that the crime was traced to King, and bit by bit, link by link, the chain of evidence was forged until it culminated in the arrest and afterwards the trial of the murderer.

"At seven o'clock in the morning on September 30, 1905,

Charles King stood upon the trap and, shortly after the trap fell, was pronounced dead."

It was this same Sergeant Anderson who was dispatched to Pouce Coupe for evidence of a murder committed in a trap line cabin well away from the settlement. The Indians there superstitiously refused to help bring back the victim's body, and it would have been a considerable job for Anderson alone. But the Mountie brought his ingenuity into play.

The deceased had been shot in the head, so all proofs of the crime lay in that part of the frozen corpse. The Mountie ingeniously solved the problem by cutting off the head and carrying it back to the station in a burlap bag or, as Dudley Shaw always maintained, in a mulligan can. Justice was thus served. K. F. Anderson was promoted to the rank of Inspector on July 1, 1915.

Charles Anderson, son of the notable Mountie, became a particularly close pal of Mel Kyllo later in Hudson Hope. Charlie, Mel, and Paul Porter used to bach together and, according to Jean Gething, "They frequently put on the most delicious steak dinners for us, Bill Carter, and their other friends; moose steaks, of course."

| *26* |

Hudson Hope Judge

▲

GRACIOUS EDITH KYLLO, wife of Hudson Hope judge and Beryl Prairie trapper Mel Kyllo and mother of four successful sons, has done as much and probably more than anyone else for the enterprising Hudson Hope Museum and Historical Society. Her work includes a history of Hudson Hope, *The Peacemakers,* which has long been a best seller at the museum here and from whose pages with her written permission part of this account of the substantial Kyllo family has been verified.

The land for the museum was donated by Jim and Helen Ruxton. The building stands next to the beautifully made Anglican log church of Hudson Hope, built with massive spruce cut a mile behind our first homesite. It was Helen, one of the Hope's first citizens, who recently unveiled the plaque put up by the Historical Society to commemorate the gift.

Edith, then Edith Edwards, came to Hudson Hope to teach. Mel Kyllo, who had originally planned to go to Fort Churchill further north, arrived in the spring of 1930, lured by talk of Canadian Pacific Railway surveys and gold rush tales. He had been prospecting with Red Kinsman in a tiny canoe; paddling, lining, and poling up the Peace and Finlay Rivers to the Omineca. When Mel returned to the Hope just before the freeze-up, the young couple fell in love almost at once and married.

It was the Depression, of course, and the time of bartering. Mel did log work, some hair cutting, a bit of freighting, and in fact practically everything else that came along. That enabled him to acquire the two cows that would be the start of an impressive herd. They needed the milk, for the little Kyllo boys were not long in arriving. One of the first things I remember about Hudson Hope was the Kyllo youngsters delivering milk among the cabins with a small cart.

Edith, with Ken and Glenn, returned home to Vancouver to await the birth of David. Mel was working with Bill Mahaffey on Brenham Flat, seeking gold which they and others found lying in a stratum of gravel a discouraging number of feet below the surface.

With what were now three sons, her sister Merna, and friend Minnie Miles, Edith returned in September. From Summit Lake, they traveled in the riverboat owned by the then famous "Goats" who included Mel's brother Peter Kyllo, Lloyd Gething, and Bud Stuart. Iva Boynton and Jean Gething had come upriver from the Portage in the heavy, long, kicker-propelled craft, so there were eight passengers for the downstream trip. The passengers elected to walk the trail alongside churning Finlay Rapids, and Edith carried the baby.

The Goats were running the boat through the fast water that swept among the rocks and bars, all the more threatening because the river was low. Unfortunately, the big riverboat grated up on a smooth large boulder and turned broadside in the current. One of the trio heaved a long rope to the passengers on shore. Edith, Jean, Iva, Merna, and Minnie exerted all their strength in an effort to tug the craft free. The one-inch line broke twice.

Desperate, Lloyd Gething who, although well built was a medium-sized youth, jumped into the water and in a moment of superhuman strength lifted the load and the boat free. As the current caught it, Lloyd somehow managed to flop back aboard. He lay almost motionless for three hours until he was himself again. In the meantime, Pete and Bud got the outboard motor roaring with one pull, safely ran the remainder of the swift water, and picked up the stranded passengers. The Goats reached the Hudson Hope Portage without further incident.

The Kyllo passengers got off before then, at Brenham Flat where Mel was digging for gold and regularly milking his cows. It was a joyous reunion, and Mel thought that young David was the prettiest baby in the world.

Mel brought his family back to Hudson Hope by pack train near the start of winter, herding the cattle ahead of them. Ken, Glenn, and young David all rode in panniers. Mel had secured nearly a dozen acres, from the Mackie Smith holdings, next to Neil Gething on the south and the Portage on the north. Here he put up a cabin, the logs of which were flattened by the same method that Joe McFarland had employed in building the Hudson Hope Hotel.

Obtaining a quarter section on the flat north of town, Mel farmed, built up an increasing herd of livestock, and trapped what had been Bill Carter's line along the Butler Range and across Beryl Prairie north. Martin was born, and success struck. Mel secured such official positions in Hudson Hope as Judge of the Provincial Court, Judge of the Small Claims Court, and Coroner.

The four boys, after youthful years of galloping around town with Beverly McFarland, Warren Gaylor, and other youngsters of the settlement, grew up to become successes in their own rights.

Both Ken and David became big game guides and outfitters, the former in the game-filled mountains north of Finlay Forks. Dave covers the trophy-rich country north of Beryl Prairie, past Chinaman Lake, and atop and along the great Butler Range. Grizzly, the hard-sought Stone sheep, mountain goat, and numerous heavily racked moose wander here.

Dave and his family also secured the former Ed Broulette quarter section on the southern shore of Beryl Prairie's Lynx Creek. I've personally harvested a number of deer and moose by this stream, from which I've landed fighting trout and even brought down a large black bear, which Dennis Murphy and I divided, a few feet from the then vacant Broulette barn.

Both Ken and Dave are heavily booked by both trophy and meat hunters, photographers, fishermen, horseback riders, all-around outdoors folk, and by mountain climbers, to the more experienced of whom the only once-scaled Cave of the Winds on the north shore of the Peace is a challenge. The Hudson's Bay Company sold Ken their former quarters in the center of town.

These Kyllo brothers, who pick up their mail and answer their phones at both Hudson Hope and at Mackenzie on the new Lake Williston, also are constantly running summer boat trips through the Peace River Valley and the Continental Trough.

Glenn Kyllo, who was mayor of the suddenly petroleum-rich Taylor until the pressure of his hardware and grocery business plus the construction profession started taking up too much of his time, lives downriver at the former Taylor Flats. Martin has been in London, England, planning gas plants for which he is a consultant. On the side, his wife and he are archaeologists.

Edith and Mel Kyllo, continuing to be most active, recently bought part of Billy Kruger's holdings where the stream long called Six Mile runs into the new Williston Lake.

| 27 |

Finlay Forks

▲

AN INDIAN BABY was so close to death at Finlay Forks that the half of the Sikanni tribe who were present chanted, wailed, and cried in their grief. On the kitchen table inside the cabin, Marge McDougall had the stricken infant wrapped in a large towel. A sterilized dish pan was ready with warm water. Also on the table, instantly available, was vaseline, salt, mustard, baking soda.

The Sikannis, back from their annual round of berry picking, had been celebrating a substantial harvest. They had been living it up with effervescent soft drinks, cans of store-bought meat, and tinned peaches and tomatoes. A young mother, in her exuberance, had fed her tiny infant canned sausage. The baby had gurgled with pleasure at the meal but had soon reacted to the strong fare. It was in convulsions, as Marge strove to clear its delicate intestinal tract.

Working as quickly as she could, Marge didn't notice that Roy McDougall, her husband, was returning with a party of sportsmen; not until they all crowded into the small quarters.

"I'm busy here," said the small, gray-haired, slender woman with a tone of authority. "You boys go into the living room, and I'll be with you as soon as I can."

One of the gentlemen lingered a little longer, obviously interested in the procedures.

"Can I give you any help?" he asked.

"You can help me most by getting out with the others and giving me working space," said Mrs. McDougall. "I think that the little thing is going to be all right, but it's still too early to tell."

The man hesitated a moment longer, then left.

About 20 minutes later, the exhausted but now quiet baby, warmly swathed, drowsed in a cardboard box behind the stove. Marge, her kitchen table cleared and scoured, appeared in the living room doorway, drying her hands.

"I hope you'll excuse me if I seemed rude," she apologized, "but things were pretty hectic for a time. Those Indians wailing out there weren't helping it any. One of the young mothers fed her seven-month-old baby canned sausage. I hope he's going to be all right. He still doesn't look any too good to me."

The sportsman who had offered his services asked if he might see the child.

"Why, sure," Marge said. "Bring him in. He's behind the stove in that cardboard box."

The hunter lifted the infant from his improvised cradle, timed his pulse, and carefully noted his breathing.

"By gosh," he said admiringly, "you've done a remarkable job. I couldn't have handled it any better myself."

"Are you a doctor?" Marge asked, wide-eyed.

"Hell, yes," one of the hunters said. "He's Dr. Wade Kelly, chief pediatrician at Temple University Hospital."

"Don't feel embarrassed, Mrs. McDougall," Dr. Kelly spoke up quickly. "I saw you had the situation well under control, or I would have identified myself when I first came into the house."

This episode, which took place in 1961, is one of many filling the diaries of Mrs. Roy McDougall who with her fur-trading husband moved in 1925 to their wilderness outpost on the Finlay River. Visiting the McDougalls first with King Gething, we have been among the travelers, prospectors, missionaries, financiers, survey crews, government representatives, miners, trappers, fur dealers, mail carriers, and sportsmen to stop at the headquarters and post office they long maintained.

Roy McDougall, fresh from his Manitoba farm where he went after being born in Ontario, originally came into the Peace River country with trapper Gus Krossa, arriving at Hudson Hope in 1925 with mail-bearer Doug Cadenhead after a trip up the ice from Rolla. Roy and Gus first became partners in sluicing some of the bright specks of gold of the Peace. Gus's becoming temporarily ill played a part in bringing that venture to an end.

Gus initially returned to Hudson Hope, then went downriver to Taylor Flats to work on the gold dredge operating there at that time. Krossa later lost the gold fever and started trapping upriver from the Hope. The last time we happened to encounter him he was happily living in a tiny log cabin near Twelve Mile Creek; that is, 12 miles west of the Portage where Jim Beattie and Tommy Stott had developed a ranch whose cabin, barn, and corral were hospitably left open for travelers heading upriver, usually by land.

Roy McDougall, too, found that fur paid better than washing the gravel of the Peace. He established a trap line and a fur-trading post at Finlay Forks, at times accumulating as much as $50,000 in pelts for Winnipeg, Vancouver, Prince George, and other buyers who flew in to bid in the spring—the season beaver pelts are especially thick in this region of innumerable mountain streams.

Marge Currie, originally of mile-high Denver, Colorado, and Roy were married in 1940. Marge, slim and attractive and with particularly impressive wide-set eyes, had come to Canada in 1926, the niece of John Johnson who put up numerous sawmills along the railroad to Smithers. With Lucile Adams who later moved to Hudson Hope, and with the wife of Charlie Pine, she had at one time run a dress shop in Prince George. So it was quite a change for her to move among the several whites and the 135 remaining Sikannis at remote Finlay Forks.

One of the ways Marge invested her time was in painting, later selling many of her works. Her first subject, interestingly enough, was a century-old squaw called Old Agnes. With her grandson doing the interpreting, Old Agnes used to have long conversations with Marge about the days when the Sikanni were a fierce and warlike tribe. One of Old Agnes's tales was about her first husband who had apparently lived only a brief time after the ceremony.

"Him very old," said the seam-faced squaw. "Him take me Fort St. James. Bad people Fort St. James. Agnes make old man very drunk. Then cut off head."

She'd illustrate the grim event with a sawing motion of her pipe, clutched stem-down in her fist. She'd laugh until the chortles turned into dry coughing.

Marge first sketched Old Agnes on paper. Then she got a portrait of her onto the back of a kitchen apron. The likeness was so realistic that Marge made several more before the mail plane came in. She dealt the first one to a Canadian Broadcasting Company cameraman for 25 dollars, her initial sale. Others on aprons went to the Murrays, newspaper publishers in Fort St. John, and to Mel and Edith Kyllo of Hudson Hope, as gifts. Later Mrs. McDougall obtained a supply of canvases, brushes, and oils.

"It's one way of bringing the Forks out with us," Marge said before the land was flooded by the government dam at the mouth of Rocky Mountain Canyon. She had completed several dozen vivid likenesses of her Indian friends, framed by the McDougall kitchen door.

Another note in her colorful diary tells of a 45-year-old Sikanni who had developed the hallucination that Marge was his father. He was a large brave and given to the habit of taking off all his clothes, no matter what the weather.

Marge radioed to the Indian Department that she was taking him out for psychiatric help, thereupon sending word to the big fellow by moccasin telegraph to come to the Forks for a plane ride with his *father*. This so overjoyed the Sikanni that he immediately shed his apparel, including footwear, and ran 10 miles through the soft spring snow to Finlay Forks, stopping only to say good-bye to startled trappers along the way.

The radio operator and his wife at the Forks had been indulging rather heavily in a spring celebration and were in no condition for a visit by a naked Indian. The wife subsequently took to her bed for several days and the couple later swore off alcohol.

During the beaver-trapping time of 1944 another Sikanni shot and killed two trappers. The McDougalls went through the ordeal of tracking the murderer, all the time knowing for certain who he was. On one hand they had to gather enough evidence for the Mountie who was on his way in, and on the other hand talk the trappers out of hanging the culprit on the spot, the *spot* being the well-frequented McDougall kitchen where a vigilante court was in session.

| *28* |

Wilderness Neighbors

▲

J. HENRY STEGE—the short, round, habitually beaming German fur trader and merchant who had long ago moved into the upper Peace River country at Finlay Forks—came downstream in 1924 and took over the Revillon Frères building near the center of the Hudson Hope settlement.

Ten years later, Stege contracted with the Gethings for a three-story frame building to be constructed with lumber from Wes Gething's sawmill on Beryl Prairie. Sawdust from the job was used between the double walls for efficient insulation. The upper part of the structure became the Western Hotel, reached by an outside stairway on the east.

A trading post and store was in the lower part of the building. Underneath was a wide and deep cellar from which I once purchased a 100-pound burlap bag of fine Hudson Hope potatoes for one dollar.

Mail had long been a problem in the Hope, especially during the freeze-up when river travel became impossible until the ice was thick enough, and again in the spring when the Peace River and its tributaries were dramatically flooded with bobbing and whirling ice floes. Mail connections were being made only once a week when my wife and I first arrived at the settlement during a cold February before the Alaska Highway was built.

Bill McIntosh became the first official village postmaster on January 1, 1913 after a special log cabin, divided into two rooms, was put up opposite the Hudson's Bay Company. Jack Mac-Dougall replaced him in August 1916.

Fred F. Monteith came into the picture in May 1921 but he worried himself out of a job only two years later, when Jimmy Ruxton took over for more than a decade. Next there was a woman in charge, Mrs. D. Eddington, who replaced Jimmy in the spring of 1934 when the beavers were prime.

J. Henry Stege took charge of the mail the next year, having quarters for it built in the upriver back corner of his large store. Afterwards the charming Miss Vesta A. Gething, a natural artist although she did not continue to develop this talent, opened a post office in the Gething home, mainly as a matter of convenience to their neighbors. She continued helping them, accompanying her work with all kinds of small favors, until 1962.

Then the present post*master,* as Mrs. F. Noreen Stubley prefers to be called, assumed competent control with a crew to help her. Visiting once with Vena and me, Noreen told us with a smile that she wasn't about to become a *mistress* for the money she was getting.

Vesta originally had her father, brothers, and Bill Carter endow the front of the early Gething home with postal facilities. That log cabin, coordinated with a bunkhouse for the men, had been built by Shorty Weber, a local trapper who was anxious to find a bride through the mail. Shorty's dreams were inspired by the success of a local provincial policeman, Ed Forfar, who had become acquainted with his most desirable wife Molly during the course of correspondence about rugs and curtains for the new Hudson Hope log barracks. Molly worked at the time for T. Eaton's who issued a large annual catalog known throughout northern Canada as "the wishing book." When the lone trapper realized that his dreams were only that, he sold the cabin to the coal-mining family.

The once-a-week mail days with Vesta were chatty, neighborly, cordial affairs when I often found myself participating in dinner or at least tea steeped from the white yarrow blossoms that Neil always had drying on the overhead joists. In fact, on many an occasion I helped Vesta and her father sort the mail, while outside the partition and closed window was to be heard the murmuring and chuckling of our sourdough friends.

You needed no current government credentials to help with the mail in Hudson Hope, and even back during Henry Stege's "administration," the heavy, balding, and friend-to-all Fred Monteith often still assisted with the postal chores. Fred was a worrier, always checking on when the mail vehicle was coming in, if Bill Carter was safe at his annual job of filling the H.B.C. sawdust-packed icehouse with blocks cut from the Peace River below, if a string of horses from the Moberly Lake side were making it across the Peace as they should, and even if a fall in the barometer augured a storm or a chinook—a northeast wind prognosticating the former and westerly breezes the latter.

One long dark winter morning a group of us were waiting for the mail which Don MacDougall had brought in the night before by pack horse. Along with me were Dave Cuthill and his associate Harry Garbitt, Joe Barkley and Dennis Murphy of Beryl Prairie, Neil and King Gething, and even Don Mac-Dougall himself. Rattling the front door had brought no response, so we made our way back of the building where the postal facilities were located and where the insulation was loose.

The soft yellow light of an Aladdin lamp revealed two plump figures, each with suspendered trousers pulled on over long-handled underwear. Both of the sourdoughs had bachelored it alone in the wilds for years. Each, probably because of that reason, was in the habit of talking to himself. Henry, it so happened, often passed the quieter moments in his store by handling both sides of a gesturing conversation.

"My, my, my, my," we could hear Fred complaining to himself as he sorted letters and packages. "Too much mail, too much mail, too much mail."

At that moment Henry entered the enclosure with the large post office key and yet another padlocked sack. He glared over his undersized spectacles at Monteith, and we could hear him muttering, also to himself, "Crazy, crazy, crazy, crazy, crazy."

Talking to oneself is a natural enough characteristic in the woods. Vena and I often find ourselves doing it. Quite a few of our sourdough friends, including Vesta and Dudley, chatted with the birds, the noisy red squirrels, and with the impish chipmunks for whom they strewed crumbs. Bill Carter, with the aggressiveness of a former North West Mounted Police constable, relished the replying echo of his own voice.

Lanky Bud Stuart was another colorful old-timer who was one of King Gething's pals. On one occasion King sent me a hurried note after his prolonged convalescence from overwork and flu, asking me to take him out to the hospital in Prince George. Bud helped me spread a mattress in the back of my Packard station wagon, and he came along with us. Vena put up an ample lunch for all and accompanied us as far as Fort St. John where I left her with Anne and Colin Campbell until I could return. Bud was to stay in Prince George with King, who came through the exhaustive examinations with only the admonition to go on a lighter diet and to get a lot of fresh air.

Anyway, one time during the worst of the Depression King had gone to Fort Nelson on business, leaving Bud and Elna Stuart sluicing gold on a gravel bar downstream from Hudson Hope and not doing too well. When King sent word to Bud that he could make wages on the river there, Bud and his wife figured that the best thing was for Bud to go. So Bud left Elna with what groceries and cash he had and took off, promising to send more money to her as soon as he could.

The grub ran out before the funds arrived. Desperate and

embarrassed, Elna took her diamond ring and the family radio to Henry Stege in Hudson Hope. She wanted to leave them as security for some victuals.

"Vot, vot?" Henry exploded. "I can't eat a diamond ring and radio."

Feeling mortified and abused, Elna tried to hold back her tears as she started out of the store.

"Vait, vait," Henry shouted. "Vhere the hell do you tink you're going?"

"I've got to find someone who will buy these, Mr. Stege," Elna attempted to explain. "I must have food. My kids are starving, Mr. Stege."

"Vhat the hell is de matter with you?" Henry said, still bellowing, frightening and bewildering Elna Stuart all the more. "Did I say you couldn't have no grub? Now git back here and git vhat you vant. I don't vant your radio and diamond. Git vhat you need."

Getting older, Henry Stege eventually began hallucinating. Remembering back to his Kootenay boyhood, the last time that Henry Stege came to the Gethings he was bewailing that someone had stolen the little hand-drawn cart which he used to deliver his newspapers.

"Dad was afraid we would lose the place when Mr. Stege was sent out, because we hadn't been able to get title to our lot on his property," Jean Gething explained, but when Henry Stege died, the government gave Jean title to the land, and everything worked out all right in the end.

Charlie and Margaret Jones were always hospitable at their cabin on the Carbon River, where the fishing has always been fine. Some of the sourdoughs began avoiding Charlie's, though, when he started keeping goats. For one thing, they complained that the cheese he made from the milk tasted like manure.

"By Jove, I don't know," was Quentin Gething's response

when the King of the River was approached on the subject. "I've never tasted manure."

Vena and I personally like goat cheese, so we always thought it was fine. But, then, almost everyone who gets past the smell barrier and tries Limburger, for instance, is usually amazed at its mild tastiness. But not many of the sourdoughs agreed with s.

Jean and Wes Gething, for example, were among the river ι velers who enjoyed the cordial welcome of the Joneses during the goat years. Jean tactfully avoided eating any of the cheese and before anyone could ask her, diplomatically volunteered how good it was. Wes, on the other hand, tried it and didn't like it but was especially effusive with his praise. Charlie and Margaret responded by sending them several pounds for Christmas.

Christmases were always great events at Hudson Hope, enjoyed by all except for the handful of Jehovah's Witnesses who do not regard the day as a holiday. The procedure was for everyone to bring his own bottle of liquor and to make the rounds of the neighbors. I'll never forget the first time when, joyous and uproaring, a mob of our friends crammed into our little 12-by-16-foot cabin.

There was talk of power dams by then, and B. C. Hydro had bought for the second dam our original homesite which the government said it would otherwise preempt anyway. Dudley Shaw, getting older, had sold us his main cabin and his 50 acres 2½ miles upriver from the Hope, cutting in half the time it took us to get the mail each week. Dudley moved to a typically trim little house on the outskirts of town, near the high cutbank there overlooking the Peace. "Deadly" long had to carry his drinking and cooking water to this new home from a well a few yards down the road.

The holiday invasion that first year gave us a happy hour, especially as Vena had our log home festively decorated. A small spruce, trimmed so that its back was flat, hung against the wall over our bunk. It was gaily embellished with some of the homemade oddities, such as three-dimensional cookies, that Vena had prepared along with other tidbits for any visitors. We put our own bottles on the table in the middle of the room. There were plenty of icicles just outside for swizzle sticks, for it had been chinooking.

Our major Christmas tree was the bearberry bush outside our latest southern bank of windows. For the snowbirds and Canada jays, Sammy the squirrel, Herman the ermine, and other lesser forest life, we had arrayed it with suet, strung popcorn, strands of wild cranberries, and more of the three-dimensional cookies.

The night before, after their expectations had been whetted by a display of colored lights which King Gething strung across the town road and wired into the Bay's generator, a party had been held for the few youngsters who enlivened Hudson Hope. King, dressing and padding himself as Santa Claus, had passed out presents provided by the community; no one was left out.

Doc Greene, who trapped and farmed near the Gates as well as practicing dentistry locally until he left for the larger town of Peace River in 1924, used to get in on these celebrations, bewildering the bushmen with sleight of hand. Doc had one of the patents on the first Wright Brothers airplane and long received royalties on it.

Bert Gregory, who had arrived from Nebraska in 1913, added his bootleg whiskey to the festivities. Joe Lermieux had arrived at about the same time but was chased out by Bert for stealing his booze. Bert was famous for his awful, but tasty, stews which one of the local ladies confided to me were "usually full of rabbit hair and dear knows what else."

Ray Fell, an early independent trucker who came to King's mine for coal, and his jolly wife Eunice made the occasions the happier when they were on hand. The four of us had once put in several stormy days alone in the mine buildings and, for the first time, Vena found someone else who, like her, was made violently ill by eating pineapple. It was Ray.

The Fells long had a sawmill at Fort St. John, another up the Alaska Highway at Mile 230, and still another one at Hudson Hope. Ray had figured out a new method of planing interlocking building logs to any reasonable size specified.

It was at one of the Hudson Hope Christmas celebrations that Dudley Shaw, who could consume an enormous amount of rum for a small man, fell into a snow bank after leaving a particularly hilarious time at the Pecks'. Snow packed behind Dudley's spectacles, and the old-timer started shouting, "I'm b! ɪd. I'm blind." Friends soon helped him up and reassured him, and the festivities continued.

For some reason, it was at one of these Christmas celebrations in Hudson Hope that Vena and I started thinking once more of the millions of other city couples who must be dreaming of a similar escape to God's unspoiled places; fantasizing and letting it go at that.

"If one advances confidently in the direction of his dreams and endeavors to live the life which he has imagined, he will meet with a success unexpected in common hours!" Finishing the Thoreau quotation, Vena threw her arms around me. "Oh, darling, darling. Dreams do come true."

King Gething came along then, and the three of us started talking about the essential difference between city and wilderness living. In the upper Peace River country, we agreed, human beings are so few that the most commonplace person takes on a very real importance impossible in the crowded places of the world.

Here he or she is not one among millions but someone rare and exceptional, and is treated that way. Everyone realizes how important he or she is in the community life, and every individual realizes that all the other people are likewise important.

"When I was sick that time," King said, "it didn't make any difference if someone had a grievance against me or if he hadn't been speaking to me for weeks. Everyone couldn't do enough for me, but Outside if anyone is in trouble, the other people walk by as quickly as they can. Here some of us may live long distances apart, but we're all neighbors."